STEPS FOR GUIDANCE
IN THE JOURNEY OF LIFE

TO Alan

ENJOY this great book on Christian
guidance.

Steps for Guidance
in the Journey of Life

PETER MASTERS

Wakeman Trust, London

STEPS FOR GUIDANCE
© Peter Masters
First edition 1995 and reprints
This new, revised edition 2008

THE WAKEMAN TRUST
(Wakeman Trust is a UK Registered Charity)

UK Registered Office
38 Walcot Square
London SE11 4TZ

USA Office
300 Artino Drive
Oberlin, OH 44074-1263
Website: www.wakemantrust.org

ISBN 978 1 870855 66 2

Cover design by Andrew Owen

Printed by Stephens & George, Merthyr Tydfil, UK

Contents

1
Does the Lord Really Guide?

'Now therefore, I pray thee, if I have found grace in thy sight, shew me now thy way' *(Exodus 33.13)*.

ONLY THIRTY YEARS AGO the question that heads this opening chapter would never have been asked by Bible-believing Christians, because the need to seek God's guidance in all the major decisions of life was firmly fixed in the minds of those who followed Christ. But the great decline of the quality of Bible teaching in the last few decades has brought with it the rejection of this precious and fundamental principle – that God has a *specific* plan and purpose for the life of each of his children, and that they should seek his direction in all the great issues of life.

The first chapter of this book will look at the new view, and prove that the old view is the true biblical position. Clearly, if we want to know about God's guidance, this issue must be settled first. Does God guide his people or not? Should we seek his will in the pivotal decisions of life, or should we make up our own minds? Seeking God's guidance does not mean that the details of his way for us will always be made known to us, but that we will conscientiously seek his direction, by appealing to him to guide and help us as we subdue selfish desires, weigh pros and cons, apply the principles of the Word, and heed the advice of godly associates.

This first chapter is different from the rest of the book because several leading contenders for the new view are named and quoted, as there seemed to be no other way of making the issues clear. Although this chapter will firmly refute the ideas of those named, nothing is implied against their personal faith and sincerity. However, this writer believes that the new view is a grave error and must be resisted strenuously as it is utterly destructive to biblical obedience and discipleship.

The 'new view' is launched

The full public 'launching' of the new view occurred in 1980, when two American evangelicals, Garry Friesen and Robin Maxson, issued their 452-page challenge to the traditional view of guidance under the title, *Decision Making and the Will of God*.[1] Overnight, this book became one of the most influential publications in the evangelical world. The authors set out to present 'a biblical alternative to the traditional view', and began by sweeping away the time-honoured teaching that God has a *particular* will for each of his children.

The same tune was soon taken up by other writers, an example being a book by an evangelical academic, Arthur Johnson, entitled – *Faith Misguided: Exposing the Dangers of Mysticism*.[2] Much of this book was wholesome material, defining and exposing mysticism, and showing how it had penetrated evangelicalism (particularly through the teachings of Watchman Nee and the charismatic movement). However, the author also fired a massive broadside at the traditional view of guidance, quoting Friesen and Maxson with approval, and

---

1 Multnomah Press, Portland, Oregon
2 Moody Press, Chicago

both misrepresenting and decrying the traditional approach.

It has been disturbing to see an increasing tide of opinion now running against 'specific' personal guidance. To some extent this has come about as a reaction to the brash claims of some believers that they have the direct leading of the Spirit to guide them, but it has been very wrong to deny God's role in guidance altogether.

In their book, Friesen and Maxson assert repeatedly that 'the idea of an individual will of God for *every detail* of a person's life is not found in Scripture.' *[Italics ours.]* But in making such statements, they show how much they have missed the point of the traditional view, for this has never said that God guides in every little detail of life, but in the major issues, as we shall explain. Friesen and Maxson dismiss almost contemptuously the numerous biblical instances of how God has given guidance to his servants, arguing that these represented unique occurrences, and were infrequent and sporadic. In other words, they are not relevant for today. We most strongly disagree, believing with the overwhelming majority of historic Christian teachers that the purpose of these biblical examples is to teach that the Lord *does* guide his people.

Friesen and Maxson dismiss well-loved texts such as *Proverbs 3.5-6* – 'Trust in the Lord with all thine heart; and lean not unto thine own understanding. In all thy ways acknowledge him, and he shall direct thy paths.' This passage, they claim, has nothing at all to do with guidance, but their 'exposition' is horrendously shallow, failing even to account for Solomon's choice of words – *ways* and *paths*. (The significance of these words will be examined later in this chapter.)

'Christians are free to choose'

The general idea of Friesen and Maxson is that Christians are entirely free to choose for themselves when they make decisions, whether large or small, provided that in making their choice they take account of the moral guidance of the Bible. Should we marry, and whom should we marry? They insist that the New Testament 'gives no clue that God's individual will determines these decisions. Rather, when these subjects are touched, the area of freedom allowed by God includes both whether to marry and whom to marry...the classic example of the principle of freedom within the moral will of God.'

It is tempting to deal with the many examples of mistaken interpretation and faulty ideas with which the Friesen-Maxson book teems, but our purpose in this chapter will be to establish the true nature and scope of divine guidance. To summarise, the arguments presented by Friesen and Maxson and other authors *against* the seeking of personal guidance from God amount to the following:

(1) Christians are regarded by God as mature adults capable of making their own decisions.

(2) God gives his people the privilege of personal choice in both major and minor matters.

(3) God wants his people to learn to make sensible decisions in the light of the moral and general rules of the Bible.

(4) God's purpose is that his people should grow in wisdom and responsibility, and not 'hand over' the decisions to him.

There is no doubt that this new view has already gravely damaged the dedication and commitment of many Christians. It is obvious that as soon as we no longer respect God's specific will for our lives, we will find ourselves at the mercy of our personal inclinations and desires. These are bound to influence our decisions more highly than they should, and we will find it easy to justify and indulge our whims. Also, as soon as we are freed from the duty of submitting to and standing loyal to God's will, we will more easily sheer away from hard callings and irksome situations. It is noticeable that wherever the new view prevails, there are fewer people toiling in the work of the Lord, fewer Sunday School teachers, fewer district visitors, and far greater attachment on the part of believers to comfort-seeking and elaborate home-building.

The Friesen-Maxson book provides us with an account of how one of the authors set about seeking a new teaching post in a Bible college, and what we see is an attitude belonging more to worldly careerism than to the ministry of the Word. It is a sad illustration of the 'do-as-you-like' approach which comes in as soon as we cease to believe that God has a plan for us. It is interesting to note that these authors believe that God calls men to the ministry in a *general* manner only, and not to specific churches, nor does he have any jurisdiction over the duration of a ministry. Under the new view no Christian worker, ministerial or 'lay', need fear abandoning his duties out of any sense of obligation to God's will.

Criticism of traditional guidance

In presenting their case most teachers of the new view misrepresent and ridicule the traditional view. One caricature of traditional guidance reduces it to three stages: (1) consult the Bible; (2) see God's signals in your circumstances; and (3) watch for good inner feelings, eg: being at peace. Such a simple plan for seeking guidance is obviously inadequate, and the traditional biblical approach goes far beyond this, as we shall see.

The most common argument employed against the traditional view of guidance claims that it is invalid because it cannot be applied to *all* decisions, large and small. Arthur Johnson, for example, derides traditional believers for seeking God's guidance on major decisions and not on minor ones. He writes: 'They struggle to find God's unique decision for their life choices. However, very few try to follow this scheme in the little decisions: which shoe to put on first in the morning, whether to cut an orange for breakfast or have juice instead.' Dr Johnson seems to think that if God does not want to decide the breakfast menu, then he will not want to direct our marriage decision either.

Another critic makes the same point about toothpaste, asking scornfully how we find out which brand or flavour God wants us to buy. He reasons that if the toothpaste decision is to be taken by us in a common-sense manner, why not all the major decisions also? On what biblical basis, these critics demand, do we distinguish between decisions for which God has a *specific* will, and those for which he does not? The answer to this criticism will be obvious from the Scripture passages which follow in a few pages.

One further criticism of traditional guidance remains to be mentioned. The critics say that if believers are inefficient at seeking God's 'perfect will', or make some vital mistake so that they miss the mark, this introduces a wrong outcome called 'God's second-best', a situation which cannot be reconciled with the concept of a sovereign God. Is this criticism valid? Is it possible to fall into an inferior course of action which thwarts God's will for us? Of course not, because there is a sense in which a believer is *never* out of the will of God. If we fail to seek the guidance of the Lord properly, and follow instead some whim of our own, then the 'wrong' outcome *is* the will of God. In these circumstances it is the will of God that we should experience hard consequences, some heartache perhaps, including the loss of spiritual opportunities, or even some harder chastisement.

It is the will of God, planned from before time began, that we should pass through experiences that will teach us true obedience, and sanctify us. Therefore, even when we are wrong we will never thwart his holy and wise will. *Romans 8.28* says – 'We know that all things work together for good to them that love God, to them who are the called according to his purpose', and even mistakes will be turned to our ultimate sanctification.

A more recent book promoting the new antagonism to divine guidance (*Is That You Lord?* by Dr Gary E. Gilley), puts great emphasis on *Deuteronomy 29.29* – 'The secret things belong unto the Lord our God: but those things which are revealed belong unto us and to our children for ever.' In a bizarre interpretation Dr Gilley claims this means that if the believer is confronted by a decision which is not explicitly resolved in the Bible, he must not seek the mind of God, but make his own decision. He says that to seek the unrevealed and therefore secret will of God would be sheer mysticism or pietism. (Another recent writer employing the same text says it would be no better than paganism.) In other words, because the name of a Christian's future wife or husband is not revealed in the Bible, that person cannot seek direction from the Lord. Both the writers just referred to are reformed in conviction, showing that this new viewpoint has spread even here, despite its unbiblical, unspiritual, and unpuritan character.

According to such writers, if we seek a job, because no modern employer is specifically named in the Bible, our future is part of the unseen, secret will of God, and so there can be no guidance for us. They repeatedly insist that God has not given any instruction in the New Testament for believers to seek his will about any of the great issues of life, not where to live, whom to marry, not even whether to seek to enter the ministry of the Word, but we believe this is error on a major scale, that will push believers further and further away from a life of obedient devotion to God.

The example of Christ our Lord

In answer to the claim that there is no New Testament instruction to seek guidance, we must obviously turn first to the all-sufficient and perfect example of our divine forerunner, our Lord and Saviour, who scrupulously carried out the precise will of his Father when he lived a perfect life of obedience as our representative. How can these authors say that seeking to follow the purpose and will of God is not in the New Testament? Astonishingly, they appear to have no theology of Christ in this matter, and this shows how far they have fallen to a 'new evangelical' view of Scripture. 'Not my will, but thine, be done' was the Lord's cry to the Father as he represented his people, and lived a perfect life on our behalf.

'Verily, verily,' he declared, 'the Son can do nothing of himself, but what he seeth the Father do: for what things soever he doeth, these also doeth the Son likewise...I seek not mine own will, but the will of the Father which hath sent me' *(John 5.19 and 30)*. These sentiments were reiterated by the Lord in *John 6.38*, and *8.28*, and they constitute the unassailable theological basis for submitting ourselves to the specific will of God for our lives, in all major ways, routes, crossroads and turnings.

The fact that the Lord's perfect obedience was an essential part of the plan of salvation shows that this is the standard required of us. The servant is not greater than his Lord (said Christ), and it is inconceivable that he would need to live in such obedience in order to be our Saviour, but that we could then do just as we pleased, as long as we kept to moral behaviour. On the contrary, the life of our Saviour is compelling for us, and we also must pray, 'Not my will, but thine, be done.'

Further proof of our duty of submission to God's will is the notion of discipleship taught through the Gospels and the *Acts of the Apostles*. A disciple was one who literally, physically followed his chosen teacher, hanging on his every word and doing his bidding. The words of Christ recorded in *John 10* apply far beyond the moment of salvation: 'To him the porter openeth; and the sheep hear his voice: and he calleth his own sheep by name, and leadeth them out. And when he putteth forth his own sheep, he goeth before them, and the sheep follow him.' This undoubtedly reflects the entire Christian life, and we surely see the words of *Psalm 23* enshrined in this tenth chapter of *John*.

The Lord's emphatic promise of answered prayer in *John 15.7* certainly includes the seeking of God's overruling guidance – 'If ye abide in me, and my words abide in you, ye shall ask what ye will, and it shall be done unto you.' We will frequently be asking, 'Lord, what would thou have me to do in my life, in my career? Whom should I marry? How should I serve thee? Lord, guide me, sharpen my mental processes, give me good insight and judgement, overrule my wrong inclinations, and deliver me from false turnings.'

Here is the Puritan concept of guidance as expressed by Richard Baxter in his great *Christian Directory*:–

'When God's ownership of you is grasped and consented to, it will make you aware how much *all* your powers of body and soul are due to his service, no earthly thing having equal rights to your thoughts, or even a glance of your affections, or a minute of your time. Keep accounts before God. Let God have what is his. Self-resignation to his glorious will is essential.'

That is Puritan thinking, exactly the view being scrapped today, but we must hold on to it, because this and this alone is real Christian living, and its loss will make for unapplied, uncommitted, unused, unassured and eventually very worldly Christian lives.

The 'roads and routes' principle of guidance

We now turn to a number of Scripture passages to establish that believers must seek the help of God to be guided in all decisions relating to life's overall pathway or direction. First, the prayer of Moses in *Exodus 33.13* is very important to us: 'Shew me now thy way.' The Lord answered, 'My presence shall go with thee.' The significant point in these words is that all the *travels* of Moses would be directed by God, and he would have guidance or overruling for his journey. Ahead lay the wanderings in the wilderness; thirty-eight years of bewildering travelling around, but however confusing and protracted these might seem to be, Moses would be most surely steered by the Lord, because he sought this.

Moses did not ask that the Lord would reveal to them their precise daily timetables, or give detailed guidance concerning all the lesser domestic and practical aspects of daily life, but that he would have guidance for their journey, route and destination. Those critics of divine guidance who scoff at Christians when they decide for themselves their daily menus, and yet seek help from God about career and marriage, have failed to observe the most basic feature of these great guidance texts. We are taught to seek the particular guidance of God on all matters relating to the *journey* of life – its crossroads and forking routes. The key lesson to be gleaned from *Exodus 33.13* is the use of the word *way* – 'Shew me now thy *way*,' which Moses meant entirely literally. The Hebrew word translated *way* refers to a *trodden road*. (The noun comes from the verb to tread.) Moses asked for the Lord's appointed path for his people.

But are we right to take the experience of Moses as an illustration of how God will guide present-day Christians? Yes we are, because the Bible says so. In *1 Corinthians 10.1-12*, Paul makes it very clear that the journeyings of the children of Israel are specifically recorded as lessons for Gospel-age believers. He says – 'all these things happened unto them for ensamples *[examples or patterns]*: and they are written for our admonition.' In other words, the pathway or route of Moses and the Israelites represents the journey of life of present-day believers.

It is not hard, surely, to distinguish between routine matters, and matters directly relating to the journey of life. Daily food obviously does not relate to the direction of life, nor to one's spiritual calling and fruitfulness. Nor does the make of car one buys relate to the course of life, though the Lord will help the search and selection in answer to prayer. Like all expensive commodities, the buying of a car is subject to the rules of Scripture. Covetousness and unnecessary luxury and expense are to be avoided, but the decision is not central to the journey of life. On the other hand, one's marriage-partner affects the entire journey of life. So does one's career. Where a person chooses to live greatly affects the journey of life, and so does the choice of a church fellowship.

In another great guidance text, *Psalm 25.4*, David takes up the language of travel, although he is quite plainly not on a journey. He uses journeying words figuratively in reference to the direction of his life, praying, 'Shew me thy ways *[lit: trodden roads]*, O Lord; teach me thy paths' *[lit: well-travelled roads, or routes]*. He uses these terms just as Moses had used them. The 'new view' promoters say that David only asks to be shown a godly lifestyle, but this is a shrinking of the sense of the text amounting to vandalism, as the psalm is full of 'journey of life' language.

In *Psalm 27.11* David again uses the same terms: 'Teach me thy *way*, O Lord, and lead me in a plain *path*, because of mine enemies.' The *roads* and *routes* terminology refers unmistakably to the *major* aspects of David's life.

In *Psalm 32.8-9* the word *way* appears once again, this time joined to an illustration of a horse or mule, which must be guided definitely and firmly by a rider or driver. Here, however, it is the Lord who says, 'I will instruct thee and teach thee in the way which thou shalt go: I will guide thee with mine eye. Be ye not as the horse, or as the mule, which have no understanding: whose mouth must be held in with bit and bridle, lest they come near unto thee.' David had sinned grievously, probably his sin involving Bathsheba, and now (as in *Psalm 51*) he is convicted of his sin, and repentant. He is no longer to be headstrong and stubborn, as a horse or mule, but responsive to the guidance of God.

Those who promote the new view of guidance say that this text is about David's *behaviour* only, and that it has nothing to do with guidance. But the point is that David had not only broken moral standards, he had also left off seeking and following God's will in the major matters of life; matters which determined the future of the kingdom as well as his personal future. He had not directed the battle, and had conducted an intimate relationship with lifelong implications. His immorality is an issue, but so also is his self-determination over where he would station himself, and what role he would undertake.

These verses, therefore, require that we submit to the direction of God in the road or course of life, which represents major matters. Just as the horse needs clear direction from its rider, so we need the guidance of the Lord in order to be of service to him. We are forbidden in this text to decide for ourselves, however wisely, where we will go and what we will do. The text is a command, a warning, and a promise, all combined.

In *Psalm 37.5* David gives us the well-loved words – 'Commit thy *way [trodden road]* unto the Lord; trust also in him; and he shall bring it to pass.' Because this psalm contrasts the lifestyle of the believer and the unbeliever, some understand the term *way* to refer to one's lifestyle, but as the 'journey of life' theme runs prominently through the psalm (the distant future reward of the righteous being referred to repeatedly) the primary sense is plainly the direction and route of life, or its major policy decisions. This is how Christian expositors have understood the text for centuries, but the 'new view' writers shamelessly tear it away.

Psalm 48.14 introduces us to another important term: 'For this God is our God for ever and ever: he will be our *guide* even unto death.' What kind of *guide* is in mind here? The Hebrew word means a driver, such as a person who drives animals or a chariot. In other words, this *guide* is a pilot or steerer; one who determines a direction. The context of the verse is the lovingkindness and faithfulness of God, who will determine the fortunes and affairs of his people all the way to the grave. To reduce this glorious language so as to make it apply solely to the guidance which God gives on moral standards (as Friesen and Maxson do) is once again to minimise the plain sense of the inspired Word of God. In this psalm the Lord has chosen a picture to describe his own role in the most important affairs of his people, and the picture is that of a guide who knows better than the animals which direction to take, and who has decided the course for the journey.

The familiar words of *Proverbs 3.5-6* bring us back to the language of the journey of life expressed in *ways* and *paths*. Solomon says, 'Trust in the Lord with all thine heart; and lean not unto thine own understanding. In all thy *ways* acknowledge him, and he shall direct thy *paths*.' The opponents of the traditional view of guidance hotly contest the meaning of the word – *direct*. They do not want to see God *directing* life's great decisions, and are quick to point out that the original Hebrew word means – *make straight or smooth*. Armed with this translation, they claim that the text merely promises a blessed life to all who keep God's commandments.

But once again their interpretation amounts to a trivialisation of Scripture, the plain sense of which shows an 'executive', superintending God, who will make the highway of life straight. In other words, if we neglect to acknowledge the Lord as supreme Governor of our lives, our paths will twist and turn in a purposeless and frustrating manner, and we will have an inefficient and unproductive journey. If, however, we renounce our own will and self-determination, and we seek his rule, then *he* will order the highway of life so that our journey is direct and purposeful. The language is designed to show that God himself will do something about the route and nature of the journey. It is his prerogative to guide in the major decisions.

Isaiah 58.11 is another great guidance promise which is taken away by the new-view writers. The prophet says: 'And the Lord shall guide thee continually.' The context (verses 6-12) is conditional. If the believer is full of compassion and mercy to the afflicted (which for us includes witnessing to the spiritually needy), then God will bless that believer with prominent influence, light, and *guidance*. Anti-guidance writers reduce this promise to the idea that if we are compassionate and good, then God will look after us, generalising away the guidance element. However, the Hebrew word translated *guide* means literally that. It would be used about a conquering king transporting prisoners into exile, in which case the conqueror determines the route – not the prisoners. The word is also used to mean govern, direct, constrain or restrict. It is a strong 'executive' word which undoubtedly means what it says – that the Lord will overrule and superintend the compassionate believer's life according to his glorious, wise, kind and perfect will.

These familiar Old Testament passages unquestionably show that the direct guidance of God is to be sought or submitted to for major decisions rather than for minor ones. The taunt that it is impossible to distinguish between decisions which God should take for us, and decisions which we should take, is made in ignorance of the 'roads and routes' language of the Bible.

New Testament guidance texts

What about the New Testament, and the bold claim of the new-view writers that there are no promises here that God will guide his people? We have already considered the supreme example of the Saviour, who submitted himself to the will of the Father as our representative. The distinction we have drawn between major matters of life's direction, and lesser domestic matters is seen in the words of the Saviour, recorded in *Matthew 6.25.* Our Lord said: 'Therefore I say unto you, Take no thought for your life, what ye shall eat, or what ye shall drink; nor yet for your body, what ye shall put on. Is not the life more than meat, and the body than raiment?' The purpose of the passage is to teach true priorities, that we must always put God first, and distinguish between affairs of the kingdom and affairs of earth. We should not be as concerned about food and clothing, or the next day's domestic routine, as about obeying the Lord.

As believers, the Lord tells us to work out the practical and every-day matters of life without fuss, as responsible Christians. We are warned not to worry overmuch about these everyday material things, but simply to be conscientious and godly in our decisions. We know the standards of the Lord, for the rules of the Word are made clear elsewhere – don't be greedy, don't be proud, don't be wasteful, don't be worldly, and so on. However, the state of the soul, the service of God, and the overall journey of a life given to him, require an altogether different level of thought, because these are not domestic matters, but great and long-term issues. Concerning these we must seek God's guidance and overruling.

Acts 13.2-3 provides a view of God exercising his sovereign direction in the sending of the first Christian missionaries out from Antioch. As the leaders of the church 'ministered to the Lord, and fasted', the Holy Spirit said to them, 'Separate me Barnabas and Saul for the work whereunto I have called them.' To past generations of Bible believers this event taught that those who are to engage in missionary service must be called by God. They expected this call to be felt by the missionary, who would have a strong inner desire for this service, and also to be ratified by the leaders of his church, who would have proved his suitability, gifts and preparation.

However, to the promoters of the new view the call of Barnabas and Saul is yet another 'one-off' event. The assumption is made that they had a special call from God solely because they were the very first missionaries. It is also asserted that their call should be seen as a unique event because God's will was revealed by direct supernatural communication, which does not occur today. The conclusion is that we are no longer to look for a personal call of God, but simply to choose, by our own wisdom, the best-suited people as missionaries.

This new 'rationalistic' approach to choosing God's servants is further justified by the strange claim that Paul did not look for specific guidance from God in connection with other missionary events, such as when he proposed to take a second missionary journey *(Acts 15.36)*, or when he took the decision to separate from Barnabas, or when he chose Silas as a fellow labourer *(Acts 15.39-40)*. It is said that Paul came to all these decisions himself, as a mature and wise Christian.

Timothy (these writers say) was chosen by Paul to join his mission partly because he impressed Paul, and partly because he was well spoken of by others. Friesen and Maxson say: 'Again, it was demonstrated spiritual qualifications, rather than a call, that proved to be decisive.' However, these authors do not appear to know about *1 Timothy 4.14,* where we read that Timothy's gift, and its use, was as the result of God choosing him, and revealing his choice to the leaders of the church. By this one text their many pages of wrong interpretation are refuted and destroyed.

It would be time-consuming to correct all the spurious arguments presented by those who so vigorously oppose traditional guidance, but the few examples we have mentioned are typical. Where the biblical narrative omits any specific mention of Paul seeking guidance, these writers feel free to assume that he did not do so, and state this as a fact. In their view, Paul did not believe it was necessary to seek God's specific will over his movements, or 'staff' appointments, but only to take sensible and wise decisions. Whenever a scripture makes it clear that God made these decisions for his servants, the new-view writers dismiss the event as a 'one-off'. But this is no way to interpret Scripture! We must protest at the humanising, rationalising and minimising of the narratives of God's Word on the part of these writers who want to be free to make their own decisions and please themselves in their Christian lives.

To return to *Acts 13.2*, we have a precedent for church life in every age, not in the *manner* by which God made known his will, but in the *principle* that his will is paramount in the ministerial appointments of the ongoing church. It was God's will that missionaries should go, and he selected the very individuals. Because the missionaries knew *God* had called them, they could be sure of the rightness of their work no matter how great the difficulties along the way. With this assurance they would not easily abandon the work. They saw themselves as men under the direct orders and the protection of the Most High God, and as bearers of his personal commission.

Paul's words on guidance

We should listen to Paul who was able to say of himself as a preacher, 'I thank Christ Jesus our Lord, who hath enabled me... putting me into the ministry.' He did not put himself into the ministry, rather the Lord did so. Similarly, he says: 'I am *appointed* a preacher, and an apostle, and a teacher of the Gentiles.' Every true minister is appointed by God, and Paul is therefore able to utter his grand words to Timothy: 'That good thing which was committed unto thee keep *by the Holy Ghost…*' Timothy had his commission, not merely from his fellow believers, but from the Lord of the harvest.

The entire narrative of Paul's journeys is the record of a ministry under the constant superintendency and direction of the Holy Spirit. *Acts 16*, for example, tells of Paul and Silas on the occasion when they were 'forbidden of the Holy Ghost to preach the word in Asia'. When they tried to go into Bithynia – 'the Spirit suffered them not.' Then came the Macedonian vision, and they knew that the Lord was calling them to preach the Gospel there. At every stage when major decisions were needed, the guidance of God was expressed, and is this not a lesson for us? No, say the teachers of the new view. Yes, says the Bible. The way God's guidance is communicated is different, because we are not apostles in receipt of direct voices and visions, but the principle remains. We earnestly pray and submit to God's direction, which comes as our minds are sharpened to see and weigh the issues, and also as circumstances are ordered to direct us in the right way. (We shall explore this more fully in later pages.)

We know that Paul's *conduct* is an authoritative example to us because several key texts command us to follow his actions, not only in the way he organised the churches of the New Testament, but in his spiritual approach to matters.[3] The message of *Acts* is loud and clear, saying in effect, 'Subordinate yourselves to the direction of the Lord in the major decisions of life and of spiritual service.' *Acts 16* unquestionably shows us Paul's concern to discern and obey God's guidance as a vital part of his decision-making.

The example set by Paul was that he must always be in the place where God intended him to be, and he constantly teaches that God's

3   *1 Corinthians 4.16; 11.1-2; Philippians 3.17; 1 Thessalonians 1.6; 2 Thessalonians 3.9.*

will must be sought and honoured. In *Acts 18.21* we find him bidding farewell to his hearers at Ephesus saying, 'I must by all means keep this feast that cometh in Jerusalem: but I will return again unto you, *if God will.*' The teachers of the new view say this means that Paul made his own decisions in the light of good sense, but was ready to submit to the ultimate will of God. They read this verse as though Paul merely says: 'I will return, but if I do not succeed then you will know my intention has been overruled by the Lord.' This, however, is to empty Paul's words of their plain sense, which is that if God directs him to return, he will do so. God's special and particular will is paramount in the major matters of Christian service.

Take the matter of appointing office bearers, where once again, we see the need to seek the guidance of God. In *Acts 20.28* Paul addresses the elders of the church at Ephesus, saying – 'Take heed therefore unto yourselves, and to all the flock, over the which the Holy Ghost hath made you overseers...' The Holy Spirit had appointed those elders, not the church. It was his guidance, not human discretion. When we appoint office bearers today, we must pray much for help and guidance as we apply the qualifications of Scripture, and weigh the suitability of a 'candidate'. We cannot proceed with the easy confidence of people who possess an executive power of decision, but only with humility and real dependence on the help of God.

Another quite different proof for the need of special guidance in the major decisions of life is to be seen in *2 Corinthians 6.14-18*, where believers are commanded to separate from idolatry and all forms of religious syncretism. The passage concludes with the wonderful promise of verse 18 – 'And *[I]* will be a Father unto you, and ye shall be my sons and daughters, saith the Lord Almighty.' The role of the father in Bible-times Eastern culture throws much light on the subject of divine guidance, because the father of the family had far more extensive responsibilities than the modern, Western father. When God promises to function as the perfect Father, his fatherhood is analogous to that of the ancient Eastern father.

This concept helps to answer the question of whether God has a specific and particular will for the direction of life's journey. The natural father of Bible times ruled the family with great authority, deciding all major matters for family members, and it was this style of fatherhood that the Lord promised to exercise in the directing of his earthly children. *He* would decide and direct in the great issues of life. When the young men of the Eastern family were out shepherding the flocks, they would use their initiative, not resorting to their father for directions over routine, day-to-day matters. They became farmers, husbandmen, traders, dyers, craftspeople and so on, experts in their own right, and in all these matters they functioned independently. But in the larger issues of life, such as where they were to live, which occupation they would learn, and whom they would marry, the supreme decider, who would always be consulted, was the father and head of the family. So it is with us in reference to our heavenly Father.

Free choice rebuked, obedience approved

The new spirit of self-determination in decision-making is strongly rebuked in *James 4.13-15*, where we read the words: 'Go to now, ye that say, To day or to morrow we will go into such a city, and continue there a year, and buy and sell, and get gain: whereas ye know not what shall be on the morrow. For what is your life? It is even a vapour, that appeareth for a little time, and then vanisheth away. *For that ye ought to say, If the Lord will, we shall live, and do this, or that.*'

Here were Christian businessmen committing a year of their lives to trading away from home, without any deep consideration of the will and purpose of God in the matter. Not only did they plan entirely in terms of the profitability of the venture, but they made up their minds very speedily, deciding to go 'today or tomorrow'. A year is a long time, certainly long enough to greatly affect one's church life and service, not to mention family life. This absence for business was clearly a major undertaking, deserving careful and prayerful consideration, coupled with a serious desire to be guided by God.

It is not enough to say that these businessmen were rebuked only for lacking a *general* respect for the sovereign will of God, as if they ought to have added the formal acknowledgement, 'God willing' at the end of their proposals. (Friesen and Maxson reduce the passage to this.) The words of James have no practical purpose unless they remind believers that they have an obligation to seek God's guidance and oversight in all the major issues of life.

James condemns believers for confident self-determination, describing it as a sin, saying, 'But now ye rejoice in your boastings: all such rejoicing is evil. Therefore to him that knoweth to do good, and doeth it not, to him it is sin' *(James 4.16-17)*. God has his own direction for us in the journey of life, and we are to apply the rules of guidance in order to honour his will and his rule. We will not always have an advance view of where he is taking us, but if we seek guidance and submit our way to him, we may be sure that his superintending hand will shape our circumstances and affairs.

A final text for our thinking is *1 Peter 5.6-7*, where we read: 'Humble yourselves therefore under the mighty hand of God, that he may exalt you in due time: casting all your *care* upon him; for he careth for you.' Sometimes the word *care* is translated *anxiety*. The original Greek word comes from a verb signifying – to draw in different directions (to part, differ or divide). It suggests a kind of care or anxiety in which conflicting thoughts clamour for attention or supremacy; in which a person is drawn in several directions at once. One translator attempts to capture this element of meaning in the rendering – 'Casting all your distracted thoughts upon him'. Behind this word lies a confusion of desires and concerns.

The same Greek word is used in the parable of the sower, where the seed which fell among thorns represents the hearer who is handicapped by the '*cares* of this world'. A battle rages in this person's mind as the lure of riches and prosperity in this world draws the heart. The 'cares of this world' are not the 'worries' of the world, but the *distractions* of the world. Paul uses the same Greek word in *2 Corinthians 11.28.* As he lists his trials and weaknesses he mentions this particular daily pressure – 'the care of all the churches'. He does not mean that his ministry of caring for the churches was irksome and painful to him, but that his mind was continuously drawn in different directions by the trials and problems of the churches.

The *care* word of *1 Peter 5* carries this sense of being torn in different directions. It refers to the divided, confused and uncertain mind, and this is especially relevant to the perplexing major decisions of life's journey. In such decisions we may cast all our distracted reasonings upon the Lord, knowing that he 'careth' for us (a different Greek word which means that he is interested in us). This does not, of course, mean that we can omit the duty of thinking through the problem carefully and prayerfully, according to the rules of the Word, but that the decision is not ultimately ours, but the Lord's.

What a reassuring teaching it is, that God has a specific will for us! It tells us just how much he loves us and watches over us, and it underlines the intimate nature of our union with him. It assures us that there is a purpose in every major stage of life's journey, every great turning point, and that there will be no wasted years or vain regrets if we seek his will. Such a thought humbles us and moves us to strive for full obedience to the will of our God.

The new approach to guidance greatly weakens the believer's realisation of the lordship of Christ. Licence and self-determination quickly become the rule as Christ is robbed of his authority and headship. We do not suggest that the new school of teachers who oppose traditional guidance intend to attack Christ's lordship, but this is what they achieve, playing into the hands of unconsecrated Christians who do not want to yield themselves wholly to the Lord.

In these days of affluence, the temptation to feather our nests and line our pockets is ever present, and the new outlook tears down the defences of believers, saying – 'Do whatever seems sensible and right to you.' Sadly, when tempted, many things (so long as they are not blatantly immoral and unethical) can seem reasonable. Under temptation, we can justify any amount of ease, plenty, leisure, recreation, self-service, and so on. The new way hands us over to the tyranny of self, and to the 'token' rule of an absent Lord, reducing evangelical obedience to the level of the nominal Christian. The fact that God has a particular will and purpose for the lives of his people is one of the greatest blessings of salvation, and a vital spur to true and living godliness. We must always be glad and willing subjects of the King of kings, for this is our high privilege and glory.

2
Six Biblical Steps for Guidance

'Shew me thy ways, O Lord; teach me thy paths.
Lead me in thy truth, and teach me: for thou art the God of my salvation;
on thee do I wait all the day' *(Psalm 25.4-5).*

THE LAST CHAPTER refuted the new, unbiblical teaching that there is no point in seeking God's blueprint or plan for our life, because he does not have one. All we can do (so this teaching says) is to make sure that our decisions are morally right, and in line with the general principles of the Bible, but in every case the choice, the executive power of decision, is ours.

This chapter, by contrast, presents a more traditional view, namely, that we are to seek *real* guidance from the Lord in all the major decisions of life, and he will certainly clarify our thinking, or overrule our circumstances. What are 'major' decisions? They are, as we have asserted, the 'road and route' decisions which concern the direction and journey of life. Career, life-partner, location for home and work, and which church to join, are all obvious examples of these journey-of-life decisions, whereas the brand of toothpaste we choose, or what we eat for breakfast, or the choice of everyday clothing, can hardly be regarded as having any influence on the direction of life's journey.

The consequences of cutting loose from God's specific will were outlined in the previous chapter, and now we turn to the biblical steps for seeking the guidance of our glorious Lord.

Step 1 – Prayer and submission

Psalm 25 has been consulted for centuries by Bible believers as a psalm about guidance. It is also a psalm of repentance, but David's need of deliverance and guidance is the uppermost theme, and we shall focus on the stages of divine guidance wonderfully delineated in its petitions. David begins by submitting his life to the keeping and rule of God, and praying for protection: 'Unto thee, O Lord, do I lift up my soul. O my God, I trust in thee: let me not be ashamed, let not mine enemies triumph over me.'

The first rule of guidance is to be learned from these words, and it is this – *submit yourself entirely to God, and pray fervently for guidance and protection.* Do not rush along the highway of life making brisk, self-confident decisions. The new view of guidance tells us the opposite, saying, 'God treats you as an adult, so go ahead and use your God-given wisdom to take your own decisions. There is no special person designated by God to be your husband or wife. As long as you make sensible and ethical decisions God will bless you. The choice is in your hands. Be responsible; but be free!'

David, by contrast, states his utter reliance upon God. Soon he will ask to be shown *God's* ways and paths, or routes and roads, demonstrating that the business-like approach to the spiritual life is not his way. To conduct our lives as though there is no higher will to seek, is to return to our pre-conversion policy of self-determination, and that is clearly wrong. We see too much of this in the evangelical world nowadays, even in the organisation of Christian witness and evangelism. Some who are supposed to be leaders of God's people plunge into new techniques and gimmicks without a thought as to whether these are in line with the rules of the Word. Sadly, it is the same with many Christians in their personal lives. They switch jobs easily, choose careers or college courses *entirely* on the basis of what they enjoy most, or move to some different region of the country just because they like the scenery. Whatever they choose to do, in matters great or small, the rule and lordship of Christ does not seem to operate much in their lives. They may often sing the words, 'Take myself, and I will be, ever, only, all for thee,' but they forget them as soon as the next major decision comes along. It is vital for us to learn early in the Christian life the glorious experience of being guided by the Lord in great decisions. The thought that the mighty God of Heaven and earth has the way mapped out for us is an overwhelming honour and privilege.

The first step always in the seeking of guidance is to submit ourselves wholly and sincerely to God, acknowledging our weakness, vulnerability and need, and in that spirit to pray sincerely for God's direction.

In *Psalm 25* (verses 4-6) David uses several different expressions as he prays for an understanding of the Lord's pathway for him. He pleads to be *shown*, and to be *taught*, and to be *led*. He asks particularly to be led into a greater understanding of the Truth, a matter we shall amplify in due course. For the present it is enough to notice that David's prayer is full of terms of submission. A genuine desire to obey God, no matter what he may direct, is often lacking in us, yet this is the first requirement in the quest for guidance. Pray over the matter in hand, also praying for deliverance from selfish or wrong motives (this will be Step 2), for eyes to see the teaching of the Word on the subject (Step 3), for mental clarity in thinking the situation through (Step 4), and that the Lord will intervene and overrule if necessary to bring about his will (Step 5). Pray also that good counsel will be given to you by others.

Praise is also an important part of prayer for guidance, because praise and gratitude for past instances of guidance build up trust for, and readiness to submit to, God's present guidance, therefore David bows his head and exclaims, 'Thou art the God of my salvation . . . Remember, O Lord, thy tender mercies and thy lovingkindnesses; for they have been ever of old.' We should praise God for the way he led the heroes of faith in the Old and New Testaments, and for the guidance of his people throughout the subsequent centuries. Then we must praise him for our own experiences of answered prayer, remembering significant experiences of deliverance, or other clear evidences of his overruling hand. Then we must entirely submit to his rule, and pledge our utmost diligence in seeking to discern his will through the biblical steps for guidance, believing and accepting with all our heart that the believer should seek –

> Thy way, not mine, O Lord,
>   However dark it be!
> Lead me by thine own hand,
>   Choose out the path for me.
>
> I dare not choose my lot;
>   I would not if I might:
> Choose thou for me, my God,
>   So shall I walk aright.
>   *Horatius Bonar*

Step 2 – 'Clearing the decks'

The second step in seeking the Lord's guidance is the crucial one of 'clearing the decks' to identify and dispose of all wrong desires, attitudes and motives. To neglect this stage is as disastrous as building a house without a foundation, and in *Psalm 25* we see how David calls to mind his weaknesses and vulnerabilities, being acutely aware of his past failings, and praying, 'Remember not the sins of my youth,' and, 'Let me not be ashamed' (or put to shame, through foolishness or failure).

We too have numerous weaknesses, and many spiritual enemies within us, including foolish desires, selfish ambitions, and covetous aims, all of which influence us greatly. How can we know God's guidance unless these are recognised and cleared out of the way? It may be, for example, that even as we ask for guidance, we have made up our minds to do what we want, and have set our heart upon some course of action. Why, then, do we pray for guidance? Because we want to fool ourselves into believing that God agrees with us and is supporting us. We want our way and the blessing of the Lord as well. As Christians we are not immune from determined self-seeking, and we can be amazingly headstrong and hypocritical, so, to be guided by the Lord, a number of possibilities must be identified and set aside.

Have we recognised and rejected any tendency in us to want something because it will bring us status and a reputation in the eyes of the world? In career decisions, for example, such desires can render us incapable of seeking God's guidance sincerely. What about covetous desires? Are we already 'hooked' by some longed-for possession? The imaginations of the heart must be honestly confessed before the Lord if we seriously want his guidance.

The writer has known occasions when true Christians have asked advice about some future step, when they had clearly already made up their minds. The pastor was meant to sympathise and agree, but seeing a significant flaw in their scenario, he felt compelled to gently point this out. It was to no avail, because the consulting friends obviously intended to go ahead anyway. Of course, a pastor is not the one whose views finally matter, but it is a shame when believers use pastors as well as other friends only as sounding-boards to confirm their plans.

Some people, though they seek guidance for the future, are inclined to seek the easy option, opting for the most manageable route through life. Others recoil from the unknown, ruling out anything which takes them into unfamiliar surroundings, or confronts them with some new field to learn. Do we know our particular weakness, and make allowance for it? Some see the Lord's will in any attractive escape route which promises to deliver them from their present burden of hardship, or of frustration or boredom. Some spend their lives on the run from one perceived hardship after another, insisting that each move is 'of the Lord'.

It is not unusual for young believers to find their hearts turned towards full-time Christian service after a few months in their first job, and in a way this is wholesome, because every believer should want the opportunity to serve the Lord. However, after school and university life the harsh realities of paid work often produce a desire to escape. Are we ready to examine our hearts, and patiently accept a period of being proved in secular work and in voluntary service in the local church before considering the Lord's work? Seeking guidance calls for self-honesty, and the hibernation of hurriedly formed ideas.

Some believers dream about a desired goal so much that they become incapable of objective thought, and are eventually convinced it is God's will for them. To project the mind into a fictitious situation to obtain pleasure or comfort is a foolish mental game which is certain to destroy honesty and objectivity in the seeking of guidance. This warning may sound harsh, but it is meant in kindness, to deliver readers from a snare in decision-making. Some believers, for example, spend time imagining themselves married to a particular person (we refer to this in a later chapter), or working in a particular profession or form of ministry, or possessing a particular kind of car or other possession, or living in a particular kind of house, and so on. All this obscures guidance and delivers the fantasiser over to fleshly desires.

To focus on a specific enemy of guidance – does our desired goal involve personal selfishness? When we trace the movements of the apostle Paul we find that his guidance often began with the great needs of lost souls, or the needs of the churches. His heart was tuned to *needs*, and he would be moved to respond to those needs. 'We thought it good,' he said, to send Timothy to visit the Thessalonian church, even though it would deprive him of a member of his team. Christians, however, sometimes make decisions which take no account of those who are in need of their presence and care. In seeking guidance, do we keep in mind the spiritual and emotional welfare of our families? We may have to clear the decks of selfish thinking in order to obtain the guiding help of the Lord.

Another problem of attitude which can ruin the seeking of guidance is the tendency to want to know all the details of our future life, and its course. This may be a feature of personality, for there are some people who cannot rest until every part of any project is fully planned and provided for. They are great organisers, but not good at trusting the plan of God, and they must learn not to demand all the details of the future. The Christian life is a life of faith in which we are being trained to trust the Lord increasingly. He guides his people in mysterious and remarkable ways, and we are not to expect a clear view on every future step. There are practical reasons why the Lord does not reveal to us all the details of our future lives, including the fact that we simply would not understand his purpose, and our constant question would be, 'Why does the Lord think that I need this experience?' Furthermore, if the Lord showed us the future events of our lives, we might run in the opposite direction like Jonah of old. If we could see the toughening phases, the humbling stages, or the chastening portions, would we submit to them? As we seek guidance, the Lord may overrule our circumstances in such a way that we come into a situation we do not like, but nothing has necessarily gone wrong. He knows what is good for us, how he will further our sanctification, or how he will refine our gifts to improve our service for him. So let us rid ourselves of any tendency to want everything to be known in advance, and completely to our liking.

Another impediment to guidance is the failure to recognise where we have gone wrong in the past and acted foolishly, bringing about the very problems which we now wish to resolve. We have produced the problems, so before the Lord will guide and deliver us, we must accept our mistakes and learn our lesson. God would be guilty of spoiling a wayward child if he led us forward without serious faults and foolishness being regretted, confessed and forgiven. So we must ask, 'Why am I in this situation from which I need deliverance and guidance?' Pardoning mercy always comes before guidance as we learn from *Hebrews 4.16* – 'Let us therefore come boldly unto the throne of grace, that we may obtain mercy, and find grace to help in time of need.' Mercy, it should be noted, comes before grace.

Psalm 25 deals with this aspect of seeking guidance, for David's past actions are much in his mind as he prays: 'Remember not the sins of my youth, nor my transgressions.' Why does he repent concerning the sins of so many years before? Has he not repented of them long ago, and have they not already been forgiven and blotted out? They surely have, but David still recalls the foolish things he had done in the past, remembering his capacity to take the wrong course, and to evaluate matters from an entirely fleshly and even selfish point of view. Now he knows only too well the snares of self-delusion and obstinacy and calls on the Lord to be his guide in his present trial.

To summarise, the second step in seeking the guidance of the Lord consists of genuine heart-searching and honest clearing away of self-delusion, self-seeking, predetermined decisions, wrong attitudes, and sinful actions. David's prayer of self-examination in *Psalm 139* may well be applied to the seeking of guidance – 'Search me, O God, and know my heart: try me, and know my thoughts: and see if there be any wicked way in me.'

Step 3 – Using the Scriptures

The third step in guidance to be derived from *Psalm 25* is that of being shown God's way through the 'truth', or the inspired Scriptures. Many major decisions, it is true, are not completely decided by the Scriptures, such as which particular person to marry, which firm to work for, or which university to attend. The text of the Bible obviously does not name present-day names. For this reason the new teaching on guidance says there is no specific will of God in these matters for the believer, but there is, and the procedures to be followed for decisions not directly determined by Scripture will follow in Step 4, and later chapters.

Scripture, however, pronounces on far more matters than we often think, spelling out principles concerning the use of time and money, principles by which we decide every large purchase, and even the leisure pursuits we adopt. Passages such as *1 Corinthians 6.12* and *10.23* are essential tests in such decisions (as we shall see in chapter 4), and it will never be the will of God for us to act contrary to his Word.

On the question – 'What church should a Christian join?' – rules for identifying acceptable churches are set out very clearly in the New Testament. Some years ago a well-known but seriously mistaken Christian leader expressed the opinion that God guided some believers to be active within the ecumenical movement, and others to remain outside, but we may be certain that if God's Word teaches *against* co-operation with false teachers, then he would never guide anyone to worship and serve alongside such teachers.

Some believers make decisions without any effort to find out which principles of God's Word bear on their situation. This writer has known of some who bought immensely expensive homes, way above their needs, rendering themselves unable to obey God in faithful stewardship. Young men sometimes apply to seminaries to train for the ministry without checking the scriptural principles which should guide them. We remember a man who applied to a college thinking that his acceptance or rejection would be a definitive sign of the Lord's will. In his case, however, the Bible spoke clearly against his suitability for ministry, firstly because he was very recently converted (whereas Scripture says, *not a novice*); secondly, because he had so far exhibited no appropriate abilities (Scripture says, *apt to teach*); thirdly because he had not yet shouldered any task in service, nor proved himself reliable (Scripture says, *to faithful men,* and, *let these also first be proved*); and fourthly because he did not have his local church fully behind him (Scripture says, *being recommended by the brethren*). In fact, not even his personal friends supported him (Scripture says, *in the multitude of counsellors there is safety*). The Bible college accepted this young man, as Bible colleges tend to do, because it needed students, and in due course he served as the pastor of a church. His work, however, was unsuccessful, and after several years of strain and unhappiness he gave up the ministry.

To check the Scriptures is an indispensable stage of guidance, and one which may involve help from pastors and reliable friends to ensure that we are aware of the biblical principles and passages which bear on the case. Which job offer should a seeker after guidance accept? In which firm would the Lord place him? Are there texts for such situations? There usually are – for example texts which urge loyalty to the church in which God has set us, and these texts may weigh against a job which involves heavy and prolonged overtime. Many texts urge us to make our service for the Lord a priority,[1] and these will obviously apply. It may be that an advertised post involves a degree of additional travel that will greatly disrupt our service in the church. From time to time this sort of difficulty is likely to affect any job, but for some it may be a regular distraction.

If people are fortunate enough to be confronted by a choice between companies, such texts may serve as powerful, perhaps conclusive, factors in discerning God's will. The light streaming from the Bible is far brighter than we often expect, and fuller treatment of how the Word speaks to different situations will be found throughout the subsequent chapters of this book. To be fair, promoters of the modern view of guidance also advocate some of these principles and passages, but only as *helps,* as we make our very own choices. The traditional view of guidance is quite different, saying that

---

1   See – Y*our Reasonable Service for the Lord,* a Sword & Trowel booklet.

these principles and passages do not merely assist us, but that they combine to show what God's will for us is, according to *his* choice, calling for our obedience. In the light of this, we use these passages very conscientiously, because they may proclaim the precise will of God.

Step 4 – Weighing pros and cons

The fourth stage in the seeking of guidance covers those decisions which cannot be resolved by the principles of Scripture, or which require careful weighing of them. This is the stage for the exercise of discernment. In *Psalm 25*, David says: 'The meek will he guide in *judgment,*' the word meaning here, *verdict* or *decision.* He then adds that the person who fears the Lord will be taught by God concerning the way he has chosen for him, although it is clear that David is not talking about direct revelation to the mind. While he, as a prophet, had been frequently blessed with direct light from God (being inspired to pen so many of the psalms for example), yet he speaks here of a form of guidance which is available to all sincere believers, and not just prophets. He refers to the meek, and those who revere the Lord, who will be helped and guided to discern the divinely chosen path, not only by studying the principles of the Word which apply to their case, but also by being helped to arrive at a sound judgement as they use their minds to weigh the situation. In the New Testament, James says, 'If any of you lack wisdom, let him ask of God.'

In matters for which there seems to be no decisive word in the Bible, we weigh the issues carefully, praying for the help of God, and as we do so, he graciously sharpens our minds and increases our wisdom, in accordance with his promises. As we weigh the pros and cons of any situation (providing we have prayed, submitted to God's will, and 'cleared the decks' of selfish desires) we will see factors which might otherwise have escaped us. This is how God's guidance works.

Some believers want to opt out of thinking through their decisions, seeking instead a direct word from the Lord. They want to 'feel led', partly because it is easier, and partly because it suggests to them that they have superior spirituality. However, we are not exempted from the thinking process in our decisions, and the faculty of the mind is not to be bypassed. God gives his people the spirit of power, and of love, and of a sound (or safe) mind *(2 Timothy 1.7)*.

In thinking through a decision we will obviously consider how the conflicting choices before us will affect our work and service for the Lord, our worship, our stewardship, our testimony, the spiritual welfare of our family, and our own sanctification. David asserts that service for the Lord is a primary issue in seeking guidance, saying that the *meek* will be taught the chosen way of the Lord, the Hebrew word meaning *the lowly*, particularly describing people who possess a servant-spirit. In *Psalm 25* it is *servants* of the Lord who receive the privilege of guidance, not self-pleasing, self-indulgent Christians who chiefly seek their own comfort, ease and prosperity. Such are perhaps more likely to be candidates for chastisement. David also prays that he will not be *ashamed*, and in saying this he is concerned above all to protect his testimony, and if we have the same concern we may be sure that our discernment will be sharpened by the Lord, who will guide us in our decisions.

This stage of guidance will also involve taking advice from reliable people, not just people we can count on to approve our ideas, for 'he that hearkeneth unto counsel is wise,' says Solomon, and 'in the multitude of counsellors there is safety' *(Proverbs 12.15, 24.6)*. When believers become mysteriously secretive and quiet, keeping their decisions entirely to themselves, it usually means they are pressing forward with objectives they know their friends may strongly challenge.

To summarise, the fourth stage in guidance is the work of diligent sifting and weighing of the issues, while praying to the Lord for blessing upon our thinking. Once again we stress that we consider our decisions not in the spirit of people who have the right to choose for themselves, but as those who long that the Lord's will should be followed. To secure his guidance, meekness, or a servant spirit, is an essential attitude.

Step 5 – The overruling of God

The fifth step in the seeking of guidance is that of watching for any circumstantial overruling by the Lord, and it is necessary to emphasise that this is the *fifth* step, and must not be placed any earlier. Many Christians have brought the traditional view of guidance into disrepute by omitting the preceding steps and leaping directly to this stage, looking for signs. This certainly is a form of mysticism, to be avoided. God does at times overrule but we dare not leave out the stages already reviewed.

How kind is our God! If we are sincere in our prayers for his direction, obedient in our application of the principles of the Word, and diligent in our weighing of the issues, and still come to a conclusion which is not his will for us, then he will point out the right course by a circumstantial intervention. This does not mean that the Lord will speak directly to our minds, but that he will firmly shut one door and open another, by his special overruling. This is to be seen in *Psalm 25,* where David uses two entirely different words for *teach.* One of his chosen words is the Hebrew for *goad,* which means train or teach. (This is the word used in verses 4, 5 and 9.) Another word (used in verses 8 and 12) refers to throwing, or shooting an arrow, or pointing to something. In *Psalm 25* it means to guide by firmly pointing out the right path. These two Hebrew words reflect two different methods of the Lord's guidance: in one case the 'seeker' is trained to understand, in the other the right way is pointed out, the former engaging our reasoning powers, the latter being more directive and practical.

Thus, David prays for two different modes of guidance, asking for *understanding* (firstly of the Word, then for wisdom to grasp his situation, Steps 3 and 4 just considered), and then, in addition, he wants the Lord to *point* to the right path by circumstantial overruling. In verse 8, David says, 'Good and upright is the Lord: therefore will he *teach [point or direct]* sinners in the way.' In verse 12 he says, 'What man is he that feareth the Lord? him shall he teach *[point or direct]* in the way that he shall choose.' Here is the intervening direction of the Lord, or his circumstantial overruling, seen so often in the life of David, and also in the life of Paul who once wrote: 'For a great door and effectual is opened unto me.' How reassuring it is when everything seems confusing, and often at the last moment, the Lord overrules so that only one way is possible. We thought a particular course of action was the right one, but then it was no longer possible for us; or we thought a particular house or flat was right, but we were gazumped or gazundered at the eleventh hour.

To bow to the overruling of the Lord does not mean that we take alarm at minor setbacks, or read significance into coincidences, for this would be a superstitious approach to guidance. When Paul's 'great door and effectual' opened there were many adversaries, but he paid no attention to the latter. Some Christians clutch at the smallest coincidences regarding them as 'signs' from the Lord, but we are not talking about 'signs', but about irreversible circumstantial overrulings.

Overrulings are often used by the Lord to lead us into situations for which we would never have considered ourselves suited, and our most careful reasoning might well lead us away from the Lord's intended goal. We think again of the experience of the apostle Paul, who would never have thought that he, the only apostle to be trained in the Hebrew university for leadership in the Jewish 'church', would be called by God to be the apostle to the gentiles. If Paul had been given the responsibility of deciding his own future, would he ever have thought himself suited to *gentile* ministry?

To summarise, the fifth stage of guidance is to recognise substantial, definitive circumstantial overrulings of the Lord. The sincere seeker after guidance may rest secure in the fact that if all diligent reasoning leads in the wrong direction, the Lord will intervene and overrule in some way, because 'none of them that trust in him shall be desolate,' and 'he will be our guide even unto death' *(Psalm 34.22 and 48.14)*. The committed believer will experience many instances of unexpected divine overruling during the course of life.

Step 6 – Assurance or unease

Our sixth and concluding step in the seeking of guidance is that of being sensitive to any operation of the Spirit of God in our hearts or consciences, either warning of a wrong decision, or assuring us that we are on the path of his bidding. In *Psalm 25*, David says of the person who is taught the way of God's choosing that 'his soul shall dwell at ease.' For generations God's people have valued an *inner peace* confirming a right course, or, by contrast, they have been cautioned by a burden of unease and uncertainty as a possible warning against a wrong one. It must be acknowledged that Christians have often brought this stage of guidance into disrepute, like the previous one, by making it virtually the only aspect of guidance. They have taken their decisions without heart-searching to 'clear the decks', without serious application of the principles of Scripture to their situation, and without diligent weighing of pros and cons. These wayward friends have gone directly to the final stage, which is certainly the most subjective stage and the most vulnerable to self-manipulation. Inevitably, their feelings have given a favourable answer to whatever they wanted.

This last stage of guidance is strictly for the person who has proceeded carefully and prayerfully through the other steps, whereas for superficial and casual seekers for guidance, it will most likely lead to disaster. The most precious spiritual benefits can be destructive in the wrong hands.

Out of these six steps or stages for seeking guidance, the last two are those in which the Lord may sound a warning if his people are sincerely mistaken in their conclusions. At the fifth stage he may circumstantially overrule to close a wrong door or open a right one, while at the sixth stage, he may give us no peace about a mistaken choice. However, the warning must be repeated, that if we claim to 'have peace' about something when we have not sincerely followed the previous steps of guidance, then we behave foolishly, if not arrogantly, forgetting Jeremiah's words – 'the heart is deceitful above all things, and desperately wicked: who can know it?' If we rely solely on a feeling of peace to confirm a right decision, then we may be certain that the heart will confirm whatever we want. Nevertheless, for diligent seekers after God's guidance, the contrasting emotions of peace or disquiet are either a valuable confirmation, or a possible warning.

It is not surprising that David should say – 'Mine eyes are ever toward the Lord; for he shall pluck my feet out of the net' *(Psalm 25.15)*. If, after honest effort, we come to wrong conclusions and head off into trouble, God will rescue us, either circumstantially, or by severe inner disquiet, whereas if we are headstrong and self-interested, then it may be God's will that we should make a bad decision and proceed into trials and discipline, for our future spiritual good.

David uses a fascinating phrase in *Psalm 25.14* when he says – 'The secret of the Lord is with them that fear him; and he will shew them his covenant.' The Hebrew word translated *secret* refers to a confidential session; a closed council where people sit down together in consultation. What a powerful way to describe the deep sense, often given at the end of the guidance process, that the Spirit of God has helped us to know his way! The 'secret of the Lord' is a special privilege of peace and communion, but it is only for those who *fear* the Lord; who want his way and not their own.

✶ ✶ ✶

Here, then, are six biblical steps from *Psalm 25* for seeking divine guidance. *First*, we submit ourselves wholly and honestly to the Lord, and pray earnestly to be shown his way. *Secondly*, we clear out all preconceived aims, and all wrong desires and motives. *Thirdly*, we honour and use the authoritative Word of God, seeking to do justice to all the biblical principles which bear on our decision. *Fourthly*, we exercise personal discernment, specially weighing carefully the practical issues in decisions not directly addressed by Scripture, and praying that the Lord will help us to see matters clearly, and to judge wisely (something that has been called 'sanctified common sense'). *Fifthly*, we acknowledge decisive circumstantial overrulings of the Lord. And *sixthly*, we desire and pray for an assurance from God about our decision, or we take very seriously any unease or disturbance of conscience we experience.

These steps are essential for all major decisions – the 'ways and routes' issues of life. For the remainder of this book it will be taken for granted that readers appreciate these steps, and they will not be reiterated. Most of the following chapters focus on specific areas of life in which God's guidance is needed, amplifying Step 3, and showing how particular scriptures apply. Chapter 4, for example, sets out the biblical principles governing activities and possessions. Though not always *major* decisions, such matters may take a large proportion of our time, commitment or money, and heavily shape our lifestyle. Failure here may turn us into worldly or self-interested Christians who will never be particularly open to being guided by God for his service and glory. It is essential to know and follow the principles of conduct provided by the Lord, however contrary this may seem to the 'do-whatever-you-want' mindset of modern culture.

3
Guidance in Courtship and Marriage

'For this cause shall a man leave his father and mother, and shall be joined unto his wife, and they two shall be one flesh. This is a great mystery: but I speak concerning Christ and the church' *(Ephesians 5.31-32)*.

NOT SURPRISINGLY, more questions are asked about finding God's direction for marriage than about any other aspect of divine guidance, especially by young people. They also seek the Lord's will about their future work, but here the mechanics of guidance seem easier to apply, and in any case, a mistake can be rectified, whereas marriage is for life.

Love is the best starting point in any study of guidance for marriage. Occasionally, even among Christians, one comes across the idea that love is not essential for marriage. Perhaps someone is deeply in love, but the other person does not feel the same way, and so an attempt is made to persuade that person that love is not vital, and that it will come with time, and this can happen. People can marry first, and then learn to love each other, just as love can be rekindled after being lost. Nevertheless, the intended foundation for Christian marriage, according to *Ephesians 5*, is love, and if we are seeking the guidance of the Lord we will not proceed without strong mutual love. But what kind of love should it be?

The present age only knows about one level of love, namely, biological love. With rare exceptions, all media interest and all popular entertainment nowadays focuses on this one level of love. Biological love, in its pure form, is the natural urge for companionship and family, coupled with an immense appreciation of the appearance and also perhaps of the femininity or masculinity of the other person. This definition disregards the corruption of biological love, which is little more than a perverted lust for nakedness or intercourse. We do not wish to devalue a human, biological level of appreciation and desire, unspoiled by lust, for it is a gift from God. However, when we speak of the *love* which indicates that the Lord may be binding two people together, we have in mind another level of mutual oneness, soaring above desires for family, or physical appreciation, and it is this level of love which is most significant for guidance. The simplest and yet the most profound way of describing it, is to call it *best-friendship* love.

Is there a growing appreciation of the other party's personality, character and ways? Is there a genuine fondness, coupled with a readiness to listen, share, please, trust and help? Is there an unusual openness to accept correction, and to take account of the other person? Is there a desire to share the Lord's service? Is there mutual inspiration, and mutual loyalty? Are there the makings of a situation in which that other person could be described as your best and closest friend in the world?

In *Ephesians 5* we learn that the love relationship of husbands and wives is analogous to the love which Christ has for his Church, and that of the redeemed for him. Christ came to die for his people, and to save them for all eternity at great cost, and in response we love him and we willingly yield our lives to him. For marriage, we should possess such a level of friendship and affection that we are ready to surrender our independence, and bind ourselves to the other person for life. Our love must be more than a biological attraction. Best-friendship love is much more outward in its flow, and possesses the characteristics in the magnificent definition of love given in *1 Corinthians 13*. It is longsuffering and kind; void of envy, self-promotion, vanity, disloyal behaviour, and selfishness. It is not touchy, nor does it fly into tantrums, or keep a mental record of offences. It does not deceive and scheme, but wants openness and truth. It also bears with all trials, is redolent with trust, and anticipates advance and happiness together. To crown all, it is genuine and consistent, not coming and going, and not inclined to fade or disperse.

Biological attraction alone can never honour the glorious terms of *1 Corinthians 13*. At its best and purest it is more of a benefit than a strength; more of an experience than a virtue. It seldom possesses consistent loyalty, and if unaccompanied by the higher form of love, fades with time.

We do not want to exaggerate the comparative weakness of biological attraction, because even this can rise to obsessive proportions and produce intense attachment and loyalty, but the higher form provides the best cement and the most profound expression of marriage, purifying biological love at the same time. Has a couple been given by God the kind of love which causes them to adapt, shape each other, and grow in the sharing of aims, objectives and delights? Only best-friendship love produces compatibility, harmony, and communication, fulfilling the remarkable words of Paul in *Ephesians 5* (quoting *Genesis 2.24*) that the man shall 'be joined unto his wife, and they two shall be *one flesh*'.

Here, then, is the pivotal question when guidance is sought for courtship or marriage: is there every prospect, every indication that this true and best friendship will be formed? Or is a budding courtship marred by constant disagreement, upsets and disappointments? Is it hard to resolve problems and settle difficulties? Are there long, tense silences, with mutual resentment and a holding out for supremacy? Is there mutual irritation, and are there wild differences in tastes and desires? If so, it would appear most unlikely that a sufficiently deep friendship and bonding could be formed. The principle uttered by the Lord through Amos holds good always – 'Can two walk together, except they be agreed?'

All life's journey the married couple will be seeking to express the closeness and harmony of 'one flesh'; one in worship, in the exercising of a sanctifying, moulding influence on each other, and in service for the Lord. Their potential for such a life must be assessed in courtship. Is the kind of friendship-bond we have described naturally and spontaneously taking shape? This is what we must look for before we should allow biological love to deepen. If biological attraction is felt the couple must hold their emotions in check in order to discern whether there is the appearance of a true, higher friendship.

A warning must be sounded here, because the illusion of a true friendship-bond can be simulated by unwise activities. It is, for example, very foolish to open one's heart too early to someone of the opposite sex in the sharing of deeply personal information. We are not thinking here of talking about sexual matters (though this would obviously be included), but about anything which is not usually shared with anyone else. We must be aware that to divulge to another person a closely kept, personal secret, such as a great hurt or failing or embarrassment, excites powerful and deep feelings, and has the effect of forging a false emotional bond with the other person. The divulger breaks through a wall of personal reserve to share close personal secrets, and the confidant then possesses a precious part of him. The difficult act of divulging releases a rush of emotion, a cathartic experience, and a bond of intimate sharing is formed. It is insubstantial, however, and will not last. If we share secrets in early courtship, we may well imagine that there is a strong bond of understanding and friendship when there is nothing of the kind. We have merely stumbled on an age-old technique for stimulating emotions, and have produced a phoney closeness. Never, therefore, cloud the formation of friendship by the early sharing of your deepest secrets, embarrassments and failures, for this may utterly confuse the quest for a genuine bond of mutual affection, which is a key pointer in the quest for divine guidance.

For the same reason we very strongly advise against close spiritual counselling across the sexes. An inappropriate bond of dependence and reliance will be formed, probably leading to an artificial courtship.

The beginning of courtship

The parallel between Christ's relationship to the Church and Christian marriage provides a sanction for courtship and casts light on the procedure. How should a courtship begin? Should the believer do nothing, and just wait for something to happen? Or should an initiative be taken, and an approach made to a suitable person? We need only ask – What did Christ do to secure his bride? Having given himself for his redeemed people on Calvary's cross, he now seeks out his people by the work of the Spirit, and woos, wins, and effectually calls each one. He must seek after us because left to ourselves we would never desire him, see our need of him, or seek him, but he reveals his saving ways to us, and his love touches our hearts.

Observing the divine initiative in salvation, we realise that the analogous union of Christian marriage must begin with an initiative, and an approach. If our attention is attracted to another person, and we are impressed by that person's love for Christ and Christian character, then we may make an approach, and talk. We will make some effort to get to know that person better, praying to God to overrule, trusting him to be our perfect Guide. Obviously, we should expel from our thoughts premature hopes of love and marriage, and certainly not fantasise ourselves married to this person. How can we sincerely seek God's guidance while, in the realm of fantasy, we have virtually arranged it, and are relishing it – even if in purity?

It is imperative that all members of a church show maturity and respect where friendships between single believers are concerned, because if all their conversations with members of the opposite sex are closely watched, monitored, talked about and speculated over, it makes the *natural* conduct and emergence of friendships very difficult. Single people must be free to associate without conclusions being drawn, and rumours circulating. In some fellowships serious-minded singles are almost afraid to talk to each other, knowing they will be married by gossip before courtship has even begun.

Apart from the obvious embarrassment, courtships have been cemented prematurely and also broken by the attention of trivially-minded, interfering Christians with nothing better to do than turn their churches into soap operas. Young people are immensely blessed wherever a pastor discourages that spirit, and where there is a deep respect for privacy, so that God's guidance may be sought and honoured.

Taking the initiative and approaching another person to ignite or test friendship is not to be done in a 'prospecting' or flirtatious way. Some young believers abandon all trust in the Lord, and rush to find courtship as though they faced doom if not quickly settled. Others fix their minds on their marriage prospect in an almost idolatrous way.

Some young believers have discovered that a succession of courtships can act as a euphoric drug, firing their imagination and lifting their mood. They would not dream of inhaling drugs, nor of fornication, but they cannot live without the warm sensations of close courtship, sharing and planning. As soon as one loving relationship comes to an end they are knee-deep in another, and almost immediately the talk is of marriage and children. Outwardly, such people appear to be pious, earnest Christians, and so they may be, but their appetite for constant courtship is self-indulgent, sensual, sinful and extremely foolish. It is also rather cruel, being painful for successive discarded partners.

In the event of a well-conducted and wholesome courtship coming to an end, the parties may be emotionally vulnerable to another, sudden courtship, and blind to even glaring signs of its unsuitability. If a courtship should end in disappointment, it is wise for those involved to give themselves ample time to recover, and the Lord will surely give 'grace to help' for this. The believer should certainly not lust or long for a constant 'love' experience. The command 'that every one of you should know how to possess his vessel in sanctification and honour' refers not only to fornication, but also to selling oneself to love and intimacy as an indispensable emotional crutch (see *1 Thessalonians 4.4*). God's pure standards, *and* his sovereign right to guide and govern us in these matters, must never be swept aside.

In taking an initiative to speak and relate to someone we need an unselfish attitude, which will deliver us from the snares just mentioned. We learn this also from the relationship of Christ to his Church, who came into this world not for his own good, but to carry out the great plan of redemption, and to save us. His work of pity and compassion was gloriously unselfish, and this should be reflected in the attitude of the believer from the very outset of courtship. It is not just a matter of what *we* want, what *we* long for, what will make *us* most happy, what *we* will enjoy, what will flatter *us*, or what will please our eyes. It is a matter of honouring the Lord, fulfilling his will, and being united with someone we love for his glory and service. Of course, it is also a matter of being fair to the other person, and being in the fullest sense a blessing to him or her. Selfish courtship is ungodly courtship, and as far as guidance is concerned, it is totally blind. It learns little about the other person, and ultimately cares very little for him or her. If courtship is all about me, my needs and my feelings, any sincere desire for the glory of God and his guidance is destroyed.

Some believers become over-anxious about marriage if they seem to be among the last of their peer group to remain unmarried, but we should not be driven by excessive pining to abandon the desire for a union based on godly consecration and real love. Do we really trust the Lord to overrule and guide? The natural desires of the heart may seek a speedy resolution, but this is a test of our trust. How will we handle the longing for love? Will it dominate our thinking and determine our attitudes, or will we pray to be able to bring these thoughts into captivity, to the obedience of our Lord and Saviour Jesus Christ? *(2 Corinthians 10.5.)*

HOW THE LORD GUIDES IN COURTSHIP
Principles from Isaac and Rebekah

The best-known passage on courtship in the historical portions of the Old Testament is *Genesis 24* – describing the finding of a wife for Isaac. It may seem strange to refer to this event for information on guidance as Isaac had all the work done for him, but the inspired record presents to us a number of important counsels for courtship. Certainly, the narrative describes a most unusual way by which God provided a bride for a special person, through whose line the Saviour would in due course be born. Because unique procedures brought Isaac and Rebekah together, the passage does not tell us precisely how we are to go about things today, but abiding principles are clear to see.

After the death of Sarah, Abraham was moved by the Lord to send his most senior servant, the controller of all his property, to procure a wife for Isaac, sending him 450 miles to Mesopotamia, where he would find relations, because Canaan was at that time a land of idolaters, and intermarriage was out of the question. Abraham's family was truly a prefiguring of the Church in the world, as God had taught him. The obvious lesson is that believers should marry within the family of God, and not into the world around, and this is explicitly required in *2 Corinthians 6.14-16*, and also in *1 Corinthians 7.39*.

1. The person intended by God

A strange feature of this narrative, already noted, is the passive stance of Isaac throughout the process. His father's servant finds his future wife, takes the initiative, makes the proposal, and brings her home. Isaac seems to sit in his tent while life just comes to him. However, the unmistakable message of this procedure is that Isaac's wife will not be chosen by his own passions or inclinations, but selected for him by the Lord. God will superintend the process, and no one will ever be able to say that Isaac interfered with or manipulated events. The Lord had told Abraham that an angel would go before his servant to lead him to the right place, and the right person.

If we belong to the Lord, we must desire the husband or wife of his appointment, believing that he has planned our lives and will guide. As we saw in the first chapter, the new, semi-rationalistic approach to guidance claims that we are free to make up our own minds in these great issues, because God does not have a specific partner for us, but Isaac's case shows that the opposite is true, and it is the same for all believers who seek his leading and overruling.

But what if we rush out and marry in haste the first believer who responds to us? Will we be out of God's will and have a partner not predestinated by the God who predetermines all things? Surely, whatever we do, his will is done, so why should we conscientiously attempt to pray for his choice? By this line of reasoning we may as well sin as we please, and then blame God for predestinating our wickedness. It is true that God's will shall be done whether we seek his guidance for marriage or not, but if we fail to honour him by seeking guidance, it may be his will to let us fall into a marriage involving much painful adjustment, so that we reap a degree of chastisement to cure us of our spiritual anarchy.

These are deep matters, and we do not want to discuss them glibly, but believers must honour the sovereign right of God to choose their partner, and they must seek his leading with conscientious care in these great issues of life. Abraham's servant clearly grasped that his responsibility was not to choose, but to recognise the guidance of God's angel. He even used the telling phrase – 'she that thou hast appointed for thy servant Isaac'. We too are not on our own in this matter, and the Lord will guide us if we apply the biblical rules.

2. Not through matchmaking

Abraham's servant was certainly no matchmaker, not having been commissioned to *arrange* a marriage, but to locate the wife of God's choosing, under the guidance of an angel of the Lord. Matchmaking is a pastime for some believers. At worst they amuse themselves by manoeuvring people into courtship; at best they imagine they are helping them to happiness, but either way, they toy with matters they do not understand, and meddle with the purposes of God. Manipulating other people's lives is described in *2 Thessalonians 3* as disorderliness, Paul referring to 'busybodies', or meddlesome people who try to run the affairs of those around them. In *1 Peter 4.15* all forms of domineering or interfering in the lives of others are condemned in these words: 'But let none of you suffer as a … *busybody* in other men's matters.' The New Testament Greek term refers to a bishop or overseer of other people's lives, and a matchmaker is such a person, a self-appointed bishop over the affairs of others.

It follows that single believers would be wise not to allow themselves to be manipulated by people who indulge in matchmaking tricks and schemes. If they suspect that they are being invited into situations which will force them into unsought, close association with an eligible person, they would be wise to avoid the arrangement, and be highly cautious of that host.

3. By honest presentation

Abraham's servant took with him ten of his master's camels, with many valuable gifts as tokens of the prosperity and security of Isaac's family. They would authenticate the account which the servant would give about his master and his son, honesty being all important.

In early courtship we must present ourselves honestly and genuinely, not acting a part, projecting a personality which is not normally ours, or exaggerating our abilities and accomplishments. Such behaviour is dishonest, God is offended, and the other person seriously misled. Isaac's approach, through the servant, was to reveal only things that could be verified, and to give assurances of his worthy intentions. The equivalent of these gifts today would be acts of kindness, and helpfulness, indicating the kind of person we will always strive to be, if the Lord encourages the relationship. Courtship is a time for love to deepen, but it is supremely a time to make sure that this is the right partner. Honesty demands that we each give a fair view of our real selves.

The celebrated novelist Daniel Defoe conceived a plot in which two people of very modest means feigned great wealth in order to 'catch' a well-born partner. Unfortunately, they caught each other, were married, and then discovered the truth. How many couples, one wonders, have feigned accomplishments, character and kindness which they did not really possess, and then, after marriage, have had to face reality? What we present in courtship must be genuine and represent our ongoing state.

The writer remembers being amazed many years ago on hearing a group of believers counselling one of their number on how to make progress in a 'match' that was forming. The counsels they gave, some in humour, but most in deadly earnest, could have come straight from any worldly group, all the usual 'play-hard-to-get' ideas being wheeled out, with many other crafty strategies. The general philosophy seemed to be that courtship was rather like fishing. You 'catch' your fish, and then enjoy it. You trap your future husband or wife, and then build a better relationship afterwards. The reality is that a foundation of genuineness is needed, and honesty is the only fair policy. We can learn nothing from the courtship tactics of the world.

4. By sincere prayer

Abraham's servant, led by God's angel, came to the city of Nahor during the early evening, and made his camels kneel down by a well. It was the time that women went to draw water, and the servant prayed very specifically that the Lord would bring the woman who was appointed for Isaac, and identify her by a certain sign. The sign requested was that she would answer his request for water with the words, 'Drink, and I will give thy camels drink also.' We should not imitate the servant's prayer today, for he was under the special guidance of God. We do not pray for signs, because we have been given a different procedure for guidance, designed for Christians in the Gospel age. Unfortunately, some believers do make the mistake of asking for signs, but the New Testament teaches that the Lord will both guide our thinking and overrule our circumstances in answer to prayer, bringing us to his chosen path.

It may be that we are eager to pray while there is no one in view, but less inclined to pray as soon as our affections are drawn to someone. Perhaps we want that person too much to pray for guidance, and apply the standards, forgetting how easily self-will and self-determination take over. Or we pray to the Lord to 'guide', but by guide we really mean 'approve'. We need to examine our hearts even as we pray, and to be sure that we are sincere in asking for God's overruling care.

5. By evidence of character

There is a lesson to be learned from the *nature* of the sign which the servant requested. He did not ask that the woman should be dazzlingly beautiful, nor for a physical indication, such as a particular movement of arms or head, but rather he asked for a response that would reveal a kind heart and a serving spirit. He requested a sign of character, and there is the lesson for us. A spiritual heart is better than any abundance of human abilities. If we have a choice between someone with many attributes but no deep godliness, or someone far less gifted, but with a warm, godly heart, we must choose the latter.

In the servant's case, Rebekah came at once, and he ran to meet her and to make his request for water. She gave him water, and went on to show the hoped-for concern for his camels. Though possessing high status in a family with servants, yet she showed herself to be humble, ready to serve, ready to toil, and unhesitating in kindness. We are reminded of a grand old Puritan maxim. 'When seeking a husband or wife, seek not according to the eye, but according to the ear.' A person's conversation reveals so much more about his or her character, interests and spiritual seriousness than appearances ever can.

6. Through time of courtship

It will seem odd that we see in the case of Isaac and Rebekah a lesson on taking our time, because the arrangements seem to be made so suddenly, and without Isaac's personal involvement. We realise that here was a unique case of very direct divine superintendence, and yet there are indications of extreme carefulness, and concern not to make a mistake on the part of Abraham's servant. It is from this that we derive a clear lesson on caution. We read in the inspired account – 'the man wondering at her held his peace.' The requested sign had been so perfectly provided that it almost worried him. Caution ruled his tongue, and he watched, waiting longer before asking Rebekah who she was. Was this really the woman appointed by the Lord for his master Isaac?

It is vital in the early stages of meeting and courtship that we too know how to hold our peace. How can we pray for guidance, and be serious about God's will being carried out, and immediately rush into a lifelong commitment? It certainly ought not to be possible for two believers to meet, propose and accept in a few days. We acknowledge that God is gracious, and the greatest foolishness can be overruled by his power. Lightning marriages which bring together ill-matched believers, can still be wonderfully sanctified, hallowed and blessed by the Lord, because nothing is too hard for him, but our duty is to pause and pray. Did we not say to the Lord at the time of our conversion –

> *Take myself, and I will be,*
> *Ever, only, all for thee.*

How can we suddenly, recklessly, give ourselves to another person, when we have already given ourselves to Christ? We are no longer our own, but have been 'bought with a price', and must therefore honour and glorify God in both body and spirit, for they are God's *(1 Corinthians 6.19-20).*

All may seem perfect – as it did to Abraham's servant – but we must still hold our peace, take no premature actions, pause, and seek the confirming guidance of the Lord. But for how long? How long does it take to be certain that the Lord has given us a firm tie, and that we are right for each other? How long before there is comfortable certainty within, and circumstantial guidance from without? How much time do we need in order to really know the best (and perhaps also the worst) of each other, be sure that we can zealously serve the Lord together, and also love and shape one another in the long years ahead? A general answer would be – the younger we are, the more time we need. For the more mature, a sensible minimum time for courtship before the arrangement of a marriage might be six months. For younger people it might be a year, but longer is better.

It is worth noting that couples are not always ready for marriage because they are not able to set up a place to live, or may have no settled regular source of income. If people are determined to marry regardless of their circumstances, one wonders how they recognise or read the guidance of God. If they ignore every obstruction, how will they ever know if the Lord is opening or closing doors?

7. By obvious spiritual enthusiasm

So far, we see a number of rules for guidance on whom to marry in the record of *Genesis 24*. We must realise that God's will is paramount, and we must be aware of the seriousness of the matter. We must pray much, and sincerely, without our minds having been made up, and our sights firmly set. We must not rush, nor allow biological attraction to take the whole matter over, so that we become incapable of reading the other indications of guidance. Obviously we must not engage in too-familiar expressions of love until a courtship is very clearly of the Lord, knowing that to do this is to throw away all sense.

We must care far more about godliness than physical attractiveness, gifts and even earthly prospects. We must see a bond of *real* friendship forming, based not on such things as emotional sharing techniques or feigned behaviour, but based on the observation of each other in deeds that reflect character.

In looking for godliness, we seek a clear love of spiritual priorities. When Abraham's servant arrived at the house of Rebekah, a meal was set before him, but he said, 'I will not eat, until I have told mine errand,' and his host said, 'Speak on.'

While this item of narrative involves neither Isaac, who was not there, nor Rebekah, it highlights the spiritual priorities of crucial importance in the quest for a husband or wife. The noble servant's first interest was not comfort and fine food, nor did he launch into hours of fascinating talk about these different branches of the family, and their trials and triumphs. His chief concern was the purpose of the Lord, and this was what he wished to speak about. Uppermost in his mind was the remarkable overruling which had led him to this place, and to the fulfilment of his special mission.

What we should most long for in a lifelong partner is someone who sincerely wants to put the Lord first in everything. He or she will be a compulsive talker and inquirer about spiritual things. Other interests may certainly engage every believer, but the Lord's things should be first and greatest, and Christian service topics ought to surface most. If we find ourselves attracted to someone who just wants to laugh, joke, and talk about earthly things, we should take a firm grip on our emotions and hold back. Pray for that believer, that by the blessing of God, he or she may change, but never say to that person (in some form), 'If you change, I will be yours.' In order to obtain that reward he or she *may* change, but only to please. Wait until the change is voluntary, genuine, deep and lasting. Always we need to ask, 'How biblical are my priorities in life? And what are his (or her) priorities?'

8. By openness to counsel

Abraham's servant soon began to speak openly of his master, and of how the Lord had dealt with him. He told exactly the purpose of his mission, how he had prayed, and how Rebekah had come and spoken to him in accordance with the desired sign. He told of how he had worshipped and blessed the Lord – 'which had led me in the right way to take my master's brother's daughter unto his son'. The point was now reached where the family were asked for their consent. The lesson for us is that while the direction of the Lord is the principal matter, other people should be consulted.

Any marriage must be a matter of free and willing choice, and it seems clear that the family asked Rebekah herself. She was certainly given an opportunity a little later to accept or reject the proposal, so we may dismiss the idea that this was an arranged marriage, and that the two families imposed their will upon her. They asked her, 'Wilt thou go with this man?' and she replied, 'I will go.'

Both parties should also be willing to listen to the counsel of their families, particularly their spiritual families, but no parent or church elder should implacably oppose the decision of two people to marry unless there is a very clear *scriptural* veto in a particular case. If we see danger signals we may warn, and even plead with couples not to proceed, but we have no power to forbid if it is just a matter of human judgement. Even in the ancient culture of Nahor the family did not claim anything like an absolute power of veto. 'The thing proceedeth from the Lord,' they said, 'we cannot speak unto thee bad or good.' And later they said, 'We will call the damsel, and enquire at her mouth.'

9. By the test of worship

Throughout the whole episode, from the locating of Rebekah to the making of the proposal, we find reference made to the worship of the servant acting for Isaac. He prays at the outset, then worships and praises God when Rebekah reveals her name and family background, and then, when the family give their consent, he bows himself to the earth and worships once again. These expressions of worship were not empty cultural acts, but sincere prayers for God's guidance, and earnest cries of thanksgiving.

If a courtship is of the Lord, it will lead to thankfulness to God, worship, and much prayer from the couple. If, however, it is more biological than spiritual, it will probably have only a scanty, token worship element, because the couple will be too taken by each other at a purely human level to think much about spiritual matters. It is obviously a positive sign when an advancing courtship promotes and deepens love and consecration to God, and genuine thankfulness to him.

10. By readiness for new roles

In Rebekah's case, when all was decided, Abraham's servant produced many further gifts, including articles of silver and gold, and garments for both Rebekah and her family.[1] They were wonderful gifts, full of significance in the culture of the ancient East. For Rebekah they signified Isaac's pledge to give himself to her, and to

---

1   See note at end of chapter

assume an entirely new role in life; and in courtship we must ask: Is there enough love and respect for true mutual submission? Will this relationship be a matter of two people struggling to get their own way, one dominating and taking advantage of the other, or will the wife acknowledge the headship of her husband, and will he gladly take full account of the perceptions and feelings of his wife?

The words 'I take thee' in the marriage service are understood too literally by some male believers who think they mean, 'I take you as my possession; my chattel, the provider of affection and support for me and my plans, and as my cook and house-cleaner.' The servant's gifts assigned dignity to Rebekah, promised every consideration, and conveyed total loyalty. If these attitudes are firmly in both hearts during courtship, then there is a strong indication that the right kind of relationship is being established by the Lord.

Are we ready for marriage? In *Ephesians 5* Paul lays down the vital duties of marriage in these terms, 'Wives, submit yourselves unto your own husbands, as unto the Lord... *in every thing.*' To husbands, he says, 'Love your wives, even as Christ also loved the church, and gave himself for it.' Is there commitment to the divinely commanded distinctive roles for marriage? Is the man willing to give himself (even to sacrifice himself) to caring for and sharing with his future wife, and will she enter wholeheartedly into her new calling?

Together for life

The bridal party took the 450-mile journey back to the household of Abraham, the rendering of the *King James Version* providing a description of unique charm: 'And Isaac went out to meditate in the field at the eventide: and he lifted up his eyes, and saw, and, behold, the camels were coming.' He was praying when his bride appeared, not fretting like a man panicking about his future. He was no 'Mr Small Faith', desperately hunting for a wife, even less was he a lusting person. We see the groom as a man of prayer, who saw Rebekah, loved her, and entered into the divinely designed union. At the age of forty he received his ideal partner for life, and the Lord's guidance was proved to be perfect.

---

1 (see page 63)

The servant had already presented Rebekah with a gold earring (or forehead jewel) and two gold bracelets, weighing – according to the experts – a fifth of an ounce and four ounces respectively.

Does God approve of gold ornaments? We believe not, for they promote vanity and luxury. But used in great moderation, and to mark special events, and to signify pledges and promises, they are surely permissible. Calvin's remarks are pertinent. 'Women who desire to shine in gold, seek in Rebekah a pretext for their corruptions. Why, therefore, do they not, in like manner, conform to the same austere kind of life and rustic labour to which she applied herself?'

4
Guidance for Activities, Possessions and Leisure

'All things are lawful unto me, but all things are not expedient: all things are lawful for me, but I will not be brought under the power of any . . . all things are lawful for me, but all things edify not' *(1 Corinthians 6.12; 10.23)*.

'Finally, brethren, whatsoever things are true, whatsoever things are honest, whatsoever things are just, whatsoever things are pure, whatsoever things are lovely, whatsoever things are of good report; if there be any virtue, and if there be any praise, think on these things' *(Philippians 4.8)*.

THESE GREAT VERSES have traditionally been taken as God's guidance on matters which are our responsibility to determine. They show which activities, interests, and possessions are right and fitting for believers, and which therefore identify the will of God in these matters. These are principles which should always be honoured in the allocation of our time, energy and money, and here a caution is necessary. The believer who is not conscientious over these matters is not usually any good at seeking guidance over major things either, because the words of Christ are true – 'He that is faithful in that which is least, is faithful also in much.'

Paul's words in the quotation above – 'all things are lawful unto me' – obviously do not mean we can do as we like, because immorality, theft, or any other breach of the Ten Commandments is sinful. Paul means that in the Christian era, by contrast with the Jewish dispensation, nothing is prohibited for ceremonial reasons. If something is moral and legal, technically speaking it is lawful for the believer, but this may not be the end of the story. Other factors may rule a thing out, and Paul proceeds to say what these factors are. In this chapter, we shall first identify the apostle's rules or tests for choosing interests, activities and possessions, and then focus more closely on the subject of leisure pursuits.

The apostle's rules or tests

As we read *1 Corinthians 6.12* and *10.23*, we note that Paul did not draw up a long list of do's and don'ts for activities and possessions, but explained the *principles* which must guide believers in their choices. This is just as well for us, as there are so many pastimes, pursuits and desirable things around today which had never been thought of in Bible times. How, then, do we determine whether an activity or possession is right for us? The apostle states that certain factors may make something wrong or inappropriate for a Christian even though it may be inherently wholesome. The test questions given to us by Paul are like a golden key with which we unlock a door of understanding and discernment for countless decisions. Here are the deciding factors as Paul presented them:

Question 1: Is the activity or possession expedient? The Greek word translated *expedient* (in the *KJV*) means advantageous or profitable. Will the activity or possession contribute to, or assist or strengthen us in our Christian walk? In both the texts where these rules are stated (*1 Corinthians 6.12* and *10.23*), the general context is our need to remain separate from sin, worldliness and spiritual falsehood, so that we live wholly for the Lord. In the light of this, Paul's question may be expanded for clarity: Is the activity or possession advantageous to me in my personal crusade to keep away from sin and to serve the Lord? Is it conducive to holy living and to witness? Or will it weaken me, place me under temptation, and compromise or spoil my testimony for Christ? Also, will this thing help or detract from my stewardship? This is the full sense of the question – Is it expedient, advantageous, profitable?

Question 2: Can this activity or possession bring me under its power? Is it something which could eventually control me, such as a drug, or even a possession which is likely to become an idol? Could it devour my attention and desire to such an extent that I shall be less zealous for Christ? Will it consume too much of my money, energy and time? Might it involve me in compromise and sin?

Question 3: Does the thing edify? Literally the question means, Does it build up? This term *edify* is usually used in Paul's epistles in connection with the *understanding*, and, through this, the *character*. Does the desired activity or possession have the capacity to increase my knowledge of God or of life in a way that will build up my character? (This may be the case if a relaxational activity leads to edifying conversation.)

If we apply the apostle's three questions to cigarette smoking, for example, we get the following guidance. *Question 1* – Is smoking expedient? Does it help, or is it advantageous for holiness, separation and witness? The rather obvious answer is that it does nothing for holy living, rather (for many smokers) it undermines self-control and patience.

Then we ask *Question 2* – Does smoking bring us under its power, and dominate us? No one will deny that smoking is addictive and enslaving. And now medical science has also established its risk to health in terms of cancer and other heart and lung conditions. It certainly wields detrimental power. It also costs the smoker dearly, taking money which should be better spent, and damaging stewardship to the spreading of the Gospel. There is also the great danger that the person who has yielded to one artificial stimulant or 'crutch', will find it hard not to yield to other forms of self-pampering. Finally we ask *Question 3* – Does this activity edify? Is there value and profit for our spiritual understanding? The answer, once again, is obvious, because smoking weakens people in times of pressure, bringing them to depend upon its effect on their mood. These questions from *1 Corinthians* enable us to test the value of things which we are considering doing or having, and are truly guidance from the Lord. A degree of latitude is sometimes to be used to arrive at a good answer. If, for example, we ask whether a game of tennis edifies, the answer will be affirmative if it serves to refresh a person in health, improving and maintaining mental and physical vigour. Excessive physical activity may have the reverse effect.

The old 'catalogue' approach

Years ago, a kind of unwritten 'catalogue' was in use among Bible believers, to show whether different activities, recreational pursuits and potential possessions were acceptable or not. There were two lists, one list headed 'worldly', and the other, 'spiritual'. Into the 'worldly' list went activities such as dancing, cinema-going and drinking, together with ostentatious, highly fashionable clothing, and (at one stage) televisions. This 'catalogue' was very widely accepted because believers knew just where they stood, and could immediately decide whether anything was good or bad.

However, there were serious drawbacks to the 'catalogue', one being that it incorporated an over-simplified outlook to leisure and possessions, branding activities and objects as either worldly or spiritual without any allowance for how these things might be used. For instance, 'wholesome' activities as diverse as athletics or serious reading could well become worse than ballroom dancing if indulged out of sheer pride, or to considerable excess, so that no meaningful commitment to the Lord's work was possible.

Also, the 'catalogue' system tended to outlaw things *totally*, in order to make matters as clear as possible, whether it was fair to do so or not. Television, for example, in its early days was entirely black-listed, people being given no scope to discern which programmes were good or bad, profitable or time-wasting.

Another serious deficiency in the 'catalogue' was that it was usually applied without any explanation as to why condemned items were wrong, so people did its bidding without knowing the principles behind their behaviour. Up until the beginning of the 1960s the 'catalogue' ruled throughout evangelicalism. Dancing was out, so was film-going, and pop music, all being assessed as worldly and sinful. But as far as the under forties (of that time) were concerned, few people had ever heard solid and biblical reasons *why* things were permitted or banned. The result was that when worldly-minded Christians began to challenge the 'catalogue', it collapsed within a single decade, many believers coming to regard it as unreasonable and unintelligent. Slowly at first, and then more vigorously as the 1960s proceeded, traditional standards were swept away with little resistance and 'Christian worldliness' took over.

The genius of the inspired teaching given to Paul is that it is strong where the 'catalogue' approach was weak. The apostle's test questions enable us to examine each proposed activity or possession closely, each person being required to determine what is right in the light of his own circumstances, motives and particular weaknesses.

Applying the tests

Let us assume that we have to decide whether we should watch something on television, visit somewhere, participate in some activity, or buy some new possession. The matter before us is not morally defective or debased, but we still need to know if it is right and appropriate for a Christian. Is it *expedient* for us to follow a proposed activity when it consumes more time than we ought to give, and will greatly reduce our spiritual service? We must be stewards of time just as we are stewards of resources, avoiding the snares of time-wasting, unprofitable activity. If we need an energetic outlet, we should not choose the most time-demanding one when there may be an equally satisfying alternative taking half the time.

The acquisition of electronic equipment needs close scrutiny, given the cost and the temptations involved. Surely it would be wrong to spend large sums to obtain a quality and performance far above that which is needed, or even of practical use. Gigantic TV screens dominate most worldly homes and also some Christian homes, virtually constituting a flag of allegiance to the entertainment industry. Certainly these are a snare, alluring adults and children into the world of soaps, sex and materialism. A smaller screen effectively says we will not come under the power of this.

Paul's tests ask:– Is a proposed possession or activity edifying and constructive enough to warrant the cost in time or money? Is it advantageous or beneficial in promoting godliness, setting an example to younger believers, or bearing a testimony to colleagues, family and friends? Are we being drawn into something which will overpower us? Will we be found coveting the trappings and gadgets connected with it? Will it consume our imagination and day-dreams? Will it erode our love and zeal for the Lord and his work?

We may feel that leisure reading may extend beyond the theological sphere, on the principle that we are to extend our horizons and our understanding of many fields, but where do we draw the line? Paul's test questions will help us to frame the right questions.

We have noted that we should weigh these matters for ourselves because what is right may differ among individuals. To extend our previous example, one person may find a particular sporting activity becomes an idol, whereas another may have no difficulty keeping a sense of proportion over the same activity. One may find relaxation and satisfaction in playing the piano, while another may find it involves too many hours of practice to maintain their desired standard. Garden activities provide ideal recreation for some, and a snare for others. Each person must take care. Whether pursuits are right for any individual depends on several circumstances, including the available time, and an individual's susceptibility to becoming infatuated and diverted from Christian priorities.

Seven further tests

A further set of standards is given by the apostle in the well-known words of *Philippians 4.8*, beginning with the words, 'finally, brethren, whatsoever things are true…' These are frequently presented as rules for the thought-life, but they actually apply more broadly to all the activities in which we engage, and the possessions we buy. Can we fearlessly apply them to our favourite pastimes and desired possessions?

'Whatsoever things are true' calls us to align all our pursuits and possessions to the Truth of God, and not to involve ourselves with anything that is actively opposed to God and his standards, such as the culture of the pop music world.

This does not mean that we have nothing to do with all works of fiction, because some may be true to life, containing profound insights, or wholesomely recreational, and even contenders for noble principles. But the apostle's rule calls us to shun works which are designed to glorify and promote a godless style of life or morality, and draw people away from the Lord. We must consider the moral basis of all things, asking if they are part of Satan's deception of the human race, an agency of darkness, and a promotional tool in the hands of the enemy of God and of human souls. Is the thing injurious to Truth?

The next phrase of *Philippians 4.8*, 'whatsoever things are honest', could better be rendered, 'whatever things are honourable, worthy or noble'. We ask, is the proposed activity or acquisition honest and open, or is it something needing to be concealed? Does it force us to be underhanded, due to embarrassment should people know that we did this, or owned this? Also we must ask if the activity or possession is honourable and dignified, worthy of our standing as

Christians. We are children of the King of kings and Lord of lords, a royal priesthood, ambassadors of God, and we must always ask if our entertainments and pastimes and possessions are in keeping with our high and holy position, or if they are banal, trivial, shallow and tainted.

The phrase, 'whatsoever things are just', requires us to be fair-minded in all our actions and judgements, because God is perfectly just, and loves to see the pursuit of this quality by his people. The test question is whether our proposed activity or purchase is right and fair, bringing into focus how our conduct affects others. Are we fair to our families? Do we choose very personal leisure pursuits, disregarding other family members? The pursuit we follow may be morally faultless, but it may be unjust to take it up to the exclusion of spouse and children. Some Christian people have been known to buy things they could not really afford, with the result that their children were deprived in some way. They did not consider the injustice when they indulged their whims.

The command, 'whatsoever things are pure', requires that everything is tested by whether it is clean, chaste, and sexually modest. What clothes should believers wear? Certainly not styles designed to be tantalising or arousing to the sexual sensibilities of others. Most screen entertainment scorns purity and vaunts sensuality and lust, and is therefore unacceptable to the believer.

Another qualifying standard is expressed in the phrase, 'whatsoever things are lovely', the Greek not referring to how lovely something is to look at, but to how love-communicating it is. All our leisure activities should conform to the unselfish, regard-for-others stand-ard of the Christian life. Does the proposed activity provide any opportunity to do good? Can I, by it, express friendship and encour-agement to another person? Will it provide scope for the blessing of someone, perhaps by providing scope for witness? Even a purely recreational leisure activity, if well selected, will yield such possibili-ties. We love our wives, husbands and children, but this standard adds to this, asking – Do we express this love not only in word but in action? Or do we become immersed in activities to the neglect of those who should be precious to us?

Are there 'love-communicating' possessions, apart from gifts to those close to us? Certainly, because Christians ideally own nothing that will bring pain or temptation to others. The wealthy believer who is sensitive to this holds back on unnecessary and excessive luxuries, not only so that the money may be better spent, but also to avoid creating a temptation and snare to others, or to provoke envy. A self-pampering and extravagant purchase is unloving and unkind particularly to young believers. Older believers, by covetous ways, have sometimes infected an entire congregation with materialism, crippling stewardship and inflating self-seeking. We need to ask, 'Are my purchases kind, or purely self-serving and damaging to the spiritual priorities and service of others?' This standard is the voice of God, and a binding word of guidance from him.

When the apostle says, 'whatsoever things are of good report', he surely has in mind activities and possessions which by their very nature create a healthy and good impression on all, including the unsaved. We ask – 'Is the proposed activity or desired possession well spoken of?' Believers are not to be characterised only for negative views, right as these may be, on the world's fallen culture, but they are to be respected for their own wholesome handling of pursuits and acquisitions. Here, then, is a test for anything we want to do or possess – is it beyond reproach, or will it cause shock, disappointment and surprise? Will it set a good example of Christian taste, humility, contentment and reasonableness? Or does it have a dark side?

'If there be any virtue,' says Paul, 'and if there be any praise, think on these things.' Virtue refers to positive quality, intrinsic strength and special merit of a moral, spiritual or health-giving kind. Can we point to something of positive value and merit in the pursuit or possession? Is character building or helpfulness to others included?

This standard steers us away from time-wasting, empty, frivolous recreations that really do little or nothing for us, and gives us a positive aim in the assessment of all choices and decisions.

Christian leisure

Throughout this chapter reference has been made to leisure activities, but what place should leisure have in the lives of committed Christians, and is there a distinctively Christian approach to the subject? Some believers reject all recreational culture, frowning on music, art, literature, and even sporting activity, and this is certainly a more commendable attitude than the discarding of standards so often seen in the modern evangelical world. But we are not disembodied spirits, and neither shall we be after the resurrection. We are created by God to relate to our surroundings and to glorify him in them. For physical vigour, nervous preservation, and personal completeness, mental and physical recreational activities are of value, and can have a sanctifying influence. While Paul says bodily exercise 'profiteth little' by comparison with spiritual exercise, it is noteworthy that the apostle frequently employs sporting activities to illustrate aspects of the Christian life, and the building of character. The discipline of the sportsman is commended, especially his determined, tenacious spirit in training. In these illustrations, physical activity receives the indirect commendation of Scripture as being useful in strengthening these qualities, and is of particular value to the young.

The greatest danger, however, is not the lack of leisure, but the tendency to want too much of it. Two scriptures urge restraint and caution, one speaking of the stewardship of time, and the other warning against selfish indulgence. 'See then that ye walk circumspectly . . . redeeming the time, because the days are evil' *(Ephesians 5.15-16)*. 'For all seek their own, not the things which are Jesus Christ's' *(Philippians 2.21)*. When leisure activities of any kind take believers away from spiritual service for the Lord (their 'reasonable service'), they become idolatrous activities. Christians are not called as God's people to pamper themselves, or to be good at play, but to be open to leisure if it serves the objectives we have mentioned, taking nothing from spiritual priorities.

The Lord's specific guidance is required for decisions which govern the major routes and turning points of life, whereas recreational pursuits and most possessions are a matter of personal choice, but the latter should be chosen by sincere application of the apostle's rules. This is authentic Christian obedience, and the necessary foundation for seeking God's definitive will in major matters.

[Further treatment of the Christian approach to leisure appears in an appendix entitled, *Tests for Amusements and Recreations*, by the outstanding Puritan, Richard Baxter.]

5
Guidance on Wealth and Ambition

'Let your conversation be without covetousness; and be content with such things as ye have: for he hath said, I will never leave thee, nor forsake thee. So that we may boldly say, The Lord is my helper . . .' *(Hebrews 13.5-6)*.

I S IT WRONG to seek advancement and promotion, and to possess wealth as a Christian? Believers face business and career decisions, and need to know if there are clear standards in the Word of God governing advancement in the world. Where should the line be drawn between justifiable, legitimate advance in wealth and authority on the one hand, and covetousness on the other?

This is a particularly important issue at the present time, when greed is one of the most prominent sins of our society. In the time of the New Testament church the great evil surrounding God's people was idolatry, but the prevailing evil today – almost the air we breathe – is a close relative – covetousness. The relationship is that both constitute an object of worship and an alternative to the true God for satisfaction and fulfilment. There has never before been a time when ordinary people in developed countries had access to such wealth and comfort. There is no point in seeking to follow God's will and purpose for the great decisions of life – the 'roads and routes' – if our lives are a mess through entanglement with the god of covetousness. The spiritual quality and fruitfulness of our future lives will depend on the stand we take on this matter.

Defining covetousness

Before we consider the advantages and spiritual justification of some measure of advancement, we must be aware of the harmfulness and subtlety of covetousness. It is such a powerful and destructive passion it can sweep away the committed, zealous stance of any believer, totally corrupting the imagination and the emotions. 'Thou shalt not covet,' is one of the primary moral demands of God. Two words are used in the Greek New Testament to signify covetousness, one meaning: the love of silver or money,[1] the other referring to the lust or longing to have more and more of something.[2] The first word highlights the aspect of *love* in covetousness, referring not just to the love of money, but also to all that it can buy. This word focuses on a strong desire for, and attachment to, possessions and also status, things which easily become a person's greatest satisfaction and pleasure, a close love-bond being formed with them.

The second Greek word highlights the *necessity* felt for these things. According to this word, once a person has obtained a certain amount of wealth or a certain position, that person cannot rest, but must have more. Such a person is always dreaming, planning, scheming and striving for more, desperate for self-satisfaction, pleasure, superiority or supremacy. In two texts where this second word is used, covetousness is called idolatry[3] because, as we have already remarked, that which is longed for is worshipped and revered more

---

1   *Hebrews 13.5; 1 Timothy 3.3; 2 Timothy 3.2*
2   *Ephesians 5.3, 5.5; Colossians 3.5; 1 Corinthians 5.11*
3   *Colossians 3.5; Ephesians 5.5*

than God, coming first in the covetous person's life.

Covetousness among believers is condemned in the strongest terms in the New Testament, being so offensive to God, and so infectious that God commands that seriously covetous members be put out of the church *(1 Corinthians 5.11)*. In various texts where covetousness is mentioned, it is ranked alongside self-love, fornication, extortion and drunkenness. Like fornication, it should never once be named among saints, says Paul, and he describes it in the famous passage of *1 Timothy 6* as the root of all evil, stirring up in the heart many other sinful thoughts and acts, and so fulfilling a Puritan description of it as 'the mother-sin'.

Covetousness is certainly a destroyer of faith, because the things which are lusted after quickly gain chief place in the heart, and are needed and relied upon instead of the Lord as a source of well-being. Covetous people always grow worse, as the Saviour indicated in the parable of the sower, where the seed sown among thorns sprang up only to be choked by the growing, encroaching weeds of covetousness. What a harrowing, depressing start this makes to a chapter! But we need to be very aware of the dangers surrounding advancement and wealth, and ready to deal with wrong motives and desires.

Factors in favour of advancement

Obviously, not all desire for advancement is covetous. It is possible to have legitimate and wholesome ambitions to secure the essentials of life, to possess a good and reasonable home, to have the means to support the Lord's work, and to exercise a ministry of hospitality. We do not follow monks, 'Christian' ascetics who have historically misunderstood covetousness. While so many of the Catholic and Orthodox popes, cardinals, patriarchs and clergy have been among the most covetous people on earth, others have thought that the only way to avoid this sin is by taking a vow of poverty, and becoming a monk or nun.

It is clear from the Bible that God grants to certain of his people considerable wealth and authority, although not by way of spiritual reward, or as an indication of spiritual obedience, because on this basis the Saviour would have been the richest person in history, not to mention the apostles, and the prophets before them. Nevertheless, God in every age has had his Abrahams, Jobs, Davids, Solomons, Lydias and Philemons. David prayed, 'Both riches and honour come of thee . . . in thine hand it is to make great' *(1 Chronicles 29.12).*

Whether believers will be approved of by the Lord in their handling of wealth and advancement will depend on their motives, attitudes, and stewardship. 'Charge them that are rich in this world,' says Paul to Timothy, 'that they be not highminded, nor trust in uncertain riches . . . that they do good, that they be rich in good works, ready to distribute, willing to communicate' *(1 Timothy 6.17-18).*

The rules for assessing whether or not we are motivated by covetousness will be presented in due course, but first we must comment on the biblical legitimacy of Christians entering higher levels of employment. Certainly, it is not wrong to succeed and prosper in career and business, or to pursue promotion. The New Testament standards set for Christian slaves apply equally to all free believers in their employment, and these encourage the most positive attitude possible. Service is to be rendered – 'in singleness of your heart, as unto Christ . . . with good will doing service, as to the Lord, and not to men' *(Ephesians 6.5-7).* A similar command elsewhere reads: 'Obey in all things . . . not with eyeservice, as menpleasers; but in singleness of heart . . . and whatsoever ye do, do it heartily, as to the Lord, and not unto men' *(Colossians 3.22-23).* These are clear commands to honour the Lord in the sphere of business and employment, maintaining interest, efficiency, effectiveness, vigour and conscientiousness. These marks of Christian character in employment will frequently be appreciated and rewarded.

However, the question arises – Will a high level of diligence or promotion detract from the believer's voluntary work for the

Lord? Is it not a case of trying to serve God and mammon? Have we not seen many Christian friends carried away by careerism, and too preoccupied with their work to make any contribution to the activities of their local church? Some may have aimed higher than their abilities, becoming so over-stretched and over-stressed that their work has entirely consumed them. But even highly competent people have found themselves in situations where they had to work all hours and travel frequently, and in these circumstances it certainly may have been better for them to have had less demanding jobs.

Numerous believers, on the other hand, have found that promotion has provided great scope for the Lord's work, and it is noteworthy that professional people and academics have been conspicuous among those who have pioneered new churches. Their contribution of time and energy to local church planting proves that a higher or more sophisticated level of employment does not necessarily destroy availability for Christian service. Furthermore, higher income levels make strong stewardship possible, enabling such people to be great stewards and constant providers of hospitality. Nevertheless, the Lord has also led many potential high-earners into lower paid careers, such as teaching, where they have influenced many young lives and taken advantage of regular hours and vacations to further the cause of Christ.

Advancement will be an advantage to Christian service only where believers are determined to maintain spiritual priorities, and not to fall into the temptations of comfort and nest-feathering. It may be argued that where there is opportunity, believers should seek a level and form of employment that will fully utilise and exercise their abilities, so avoiding much frustration, boredom and tension, and hopefully reaping greater fulfilment, well-being and energy for the Lord's work.

We must reject as utterly unbiblical the false teaching of many (though by no means all) charismatics that Christians are meant to have prosperity, and God will make them wealthy according to their faith (not to mention their liberal contribution to the enrichment of their preachers). The wealth of many charismatic preachers is a scandal, serving only to demonstrate their hypocrisy, and how much Paul's words apply to them – 'whose God is their belly, and whose glory is in their shame, who mind earthly things' *(Philippians 3.19)*.

What is our motive? – Five searching tests

As far as guidance is concerned, if we are confronted by major decisions about future career or promotion, or where to work, how can we tell if our inclinations and desires are reasonable, or covetous? The following tests should identify the point at which a desire becomes covetous, and although these tests may seem to be similar, there are important distinctions between them. The tests would also apply to the buying of houses, cars, appliances or anything else of high cost or 'visibility'.

1. The first test challenges our attitude, stating: when the heart is set upon promotion, elevation, or the accumulation of substance *for its own sake* it is covetousness. In the case of promotion, if believers recognise, with genuine humility, that God has given them certain capacities which ought to be exercised, they should work for promotion. Their main objectives will be to utilise the gifts God has given them in order to house and provide for their family, and strengthen their stewardship, and show compassion to others. These objectives are not of themselves covetous. But if promotion is wanted for greater status, esteem and respect from others, and for power over others, then the boundary to covetousness has been crossed, covetousness arising from the spirit in which our objectives are pursued.

What drives us on? What gives us the energy and enthusiasm to achieve our goals, whether by further study or overtime? If status or substance are in view, and these are the incentives that keep us going, then we have fallen into covetousness and self-seeking.

2. The second test is similar, suggesting that we fall into covetousness when the possession of money or status (or academic accomplishment) becomes the *key to happiness and contentment.* Do we look to these things to make life worthwhile, and are we miserable and out-of-sorts if there is no prospect of getting them? If so, we are obviously controlled by covetousness, because true believers seek their happiness and contentment in Christ and his service and people, and, of course, in their families, not in material things. It is true that an element of legitimate pleasure may be derived from the things we possess, and a degree of fulfilment may come from high responsibilities, but when we *depend* upon such earthly sources for our happiness and joy, we have fallen into covetousness.

Can we tell if this has happened to us? Simple questions reveal the truth. If we are depressed do we go out and buy something? Do we seek uplift by day-dreaming about things we hope to have? Do we plan colour schemes, home extensions, new cars, or things of that kind? Do we fantasise about promotion or higher status in life? When these things become our chief means of escape from heaviness of spirit and our only route to an improved mood, then we are in the grip of covetousness. When substance and status are craved as the only effective solution to life's problems and situations, we are in trouble.

If we are in normal mental health there is no temptation or need which the Lord cannot lift us from, or strengthen us to get through; and no situation that he cannot enable us to bear, or deliver us from, if that is his will. God may use material resources to deliver us from difficult situations, but we must look to *him*, not to those earthly resources. Earthly things and status must never become our hope, and our key to satisfaction, for the Word says, 'Trust in him at all times; ye people.'

3. The third test defines covetousness as the sin into which we fall when possessions, position or promotion or academic achievement engage our energies *at the expense of the Lord's service.* If the earning of money, attention to business affairs, or additional studies for promotion, take us regularly and long term from service of the Lord, we have probably become covetous. Obviously, this would not apply to defined periods for further or vocational training, or to 'emergency' seasons when exceptional demands are imposed on us, but if pursuit of advancement takes us from the fellowship of God's people, from worship, or from being chiefly concerned with his cause in a repeated, or never-ending manner, it is likely that covetousness is ruling over right Christian priorities.

To amplify the exception just mentioned, it would surely be acceptable to pursue a set period of study or training for a limited span of years, with a definite objective and termination. It may equally happen that a Christian has to go through a difficult passage in his business or professional life, but it is not going to last. Abnormal hours may have to be worked for a phase in the 'career structure', or to establish something in a business of our own. It is for a limited time only, and then a fuller commitment to the service of the Lord will be resumed. But when our *normal lives* (by our own choice) become so committed to the things of this world that we, as Christians, are constantly and willingly stolen from the Lord and his service, we are probably in the grip of covetousness. We must fear the possibility of being swallowed up by self-consideration and covetousness, never forgetting that the heart is deceitful above all things and desperately wicked. It so easily justifies earthly aspirations.

4. The fourth test reveals a clear case of covetousness when the desire for substance and status is for *self-exaltation*. This is a desire to have certain things in order to be seen to be above other people, or to have accomplished more, and be superior to them. Pride joins hands with covetousness to create a longing for position and possessions in order that the possessor may feel especially satisfied and significant.

5. The fifth test finds covetousness when the person is driven by a passion for *wanting more and still more* of something. It may be that for many months the heart has been set on attaining some objective, or acquiring some possession, and now the longing has been met and the desired thing achieved. But very soon it fails to satisfy, emptiness and unease envelops mind and heart, and another objective quickly takes shape in the imagination. Through life the restless person lurches from scheme to scheme, project to project, possession to possession, never content, and always aiming forward. Life is energised by dreaming, anticipating, planning, achieving, gloating, and then returning to the beginning of the process. Always, the person must have something else; something more. Such a life is either immensely pleasurable, or burningly necessary, but it is altogether earthly and covetous. Do we always need more? Is this the real purpose of our quest for a new job or house or car or qualification?

A brief summary of tests will help at this point to determine whether our aims are right and valid.

1. If the love of substance, status or possessions is the driving force and motivating factor in our lives, our aims are covetous.

2. If these things are in practice the key to our happiness, the way to gain uplift, the chief source of relief, and the only answer to our problems, then our aims are covetous.

3. If the pursuit of status and possessions is carried on at the expense of Christian service, our aims are covetous.

4. If advancement is sought for self-exaltation and esteem from others, our aims are certainly covetous.

5. If the desire for 'more and better' has secured such a grip on the heart, that we always need something more, and move restlessly from one accomplishment to another, then our aims are covetous.

Antidotes to covetousness

After reading these characteristics of covetousness we may wonder if anyone can legitimately seek promotion or advancement, because fallen nature is bound to intrude. However, there are biblical antidotes to covetousness, which now follow.

1. The first antidote to covetousness is to *pray* against it, and frequently. We particularly press this advice upon those who are given by God the responsibility of stewarding wealth, and also those who are placed in high positions. Believers must pray earnestly, honestly and self-searchingly for deliverance from the snare of covetousness, in the spirit of Paul's warning, 'O man of God, *flee* these things.'

2. A second antidote to covetousness is exemplified in the life of the apostle Paul, who practised *self-discipline and self-denial.* Was there ever a person in such a position of opportunity for power and plenty as Paul? He was called to be an instrument for the conversion of very large numbers of people, including the rich. Such a man could surely be tempted to pursue influence and esteem in a wrong and covetous way, because many people would have given Paul whatever he wanted or needed, out of love and appreciation. If he had been inclined to rein back his labours to secure more comfort, and to be less rigorous in requiring a high standard of practical godliness and evangelism in the churches, he could have amassed wealth just as some of the 'megachurch' pastors do today.

We certainly see in Scripture hints of the enormous love and gratitude that many held for him. Why is it that Paul is able to say to Philemon (when he returned Onesimus, the runaway slave), 'If he hath wronged thee, or oweth thee ought, put that on mine account'? Philemon owed an immense debt of gratitude to Paul, and the apostle seems to say, 'Remember all those things you would have given me? – please regard this poor slave's misdemeanours as debited from those.' Elsewhere Paul speaks of certain procedures he adopted to guard against various temptations, particularly mentioning how he 'kept under' his body (see *1 Corinthians 9.25-27*). We give ourselves no chance at all against the temptations of self-seeking and covetousness if we never practise self-denial or self-discipline, and the apostle commends it to us.

Paul seems to say that there were many things he could have indulged in or possessed – 'But I keep a tight rein on myself; I practise self-denial; I do not unnecessarily give way to myself or weaken myself by pampering the body.' Paul did not take a vow of poverty or wear a hair shirt, and certainly did not submit himself to deliberate hardship or self-affliction like a medieval monk, but he was very firm with himself. By keeping a firm rein on ourselves in the matter of possessions, we too may deliver ourselves from much temptation. If, on the other hand, we pamper ourselves with many small self-indulgences, we must not be surprised if we become weak, and fall to bigger temptations.

If you have substance, never let it spoil you. Steward it, invest it, do what you think right with it, but never let it take over your heart, rule you, and become essential to you for your well-being. By all means own things which bring beauty and enjoyment into life, but do not acquire too many of those things, because if you do, you will place yourself into a terrible snare, and weaken yourself for Satan's next major attempt to bring you further still under the power of covetousness. Be firm to draw the line on unjustifiable purchases and pleasures, or things of unjustifiably high quality. If the apostle Paul found it necessary to keep under his body and to set limits upon himself, who are we to imagine that we can survive the scourge of covetousness without such discipline? We are not urging total austerity. Balance is necessary, but we must avoid giving way to the flesh, so that we always have the very best that we can afford, and never curb our desires.

3. A third antidote to covetousness is *generosity*. A large-hearted giver who liberally stewards to the Lord's work will not stumble so easily into self-seeking. In times of prosperity and material advance, the believer must ask, 'For whose sake has the Lord prospered me, for mine, or for his?'[4] The Lord has no need of anything we can give, but he has made us fellow-heirs with Christ, and given us the

---

4   See – *Tithing, the Privilege of Christian Stewardship*, a Sword & Trowel booklet.

greatest privilege on earth, that of sharing in the extension of the kingdom of the Saviour, to whom we owe everything.

4. A fourth antidote to covetousness comes from *Colossians 3.2* – 'Set your affection on things above, not on things on the earth.' The conscious *cultivation of spiritual interests* will deliver us from covetous attraction to earthly possessions and worldly status. Whenever the eyes of the mind focus on material things, and the imagination roves and relishes in the streets of Vanity Fair, we should wrench our thoughts away, and divert them to things that really matter, to spiritual issues. There are always better things to think about. Is there not something that we should be planning or preparing for the Lord? Is there nothing *spiritual* to remember, read about, reflect on and rejoice in? Are there no people for whom we should be concerned? Is there no one to seek out, encourage, comfort, perhaps this very moment telephone, in the name of the Lord? The possibilities are unending. Have we nothing edifying to read or study? Have we no one to pray for?

If we are really absorbed in the Lord and his Word, there will be little scope for our emotional and mental energies to run after worldly things. If we seek our families, colleagues and friends for him, and if we are passionately involved in the progress of the Gospel in every place, we will be safely preserved from the great snare of covetousness.

Let us train ourselves to desire, cherish and love spiritual blessings first; then it will be possible for us to keep earthly blessings in perspective. We need the spirit of the psalmist who said, 'A day in thy courts is better than a thousand.' Our tastes need to be so enlivened and refined by the Lord, that the Lord's Day, the Lord's house, the Lord's ways, and the fellowship and concerns of the Lord's people are always at the top of our list of interests. If this is true of us, we will not stumble easily into covetousness.

5. A fifth antidote to covetousness is in the verse with which this chapter began – 'Let your conversation be without covetousness;

and be content with such things as ye have.' Elsewhere, the apostle Paul says, 'I have learned, in whatsoever state I am, therewith to be content.' The *practice of contentment* is a great antidote. This does not mean that we never seek advancement or promotion, but that our present condition, however lowly, does not chafe and aggravate us, causing us to become restive, frustrated and even resentful.

We may look ahead, and work on, seeking to advance and increase, but not out of pained dissatisfaction with our present state. On the contrary, the believer takes care to give thanks for and appreciate all that the Lord has done, and all that he has provided. Husband, wife, children and friends are especially to be included in this. Life has countless blessings (if only we have eyes to see) vastly greater than material wealth. If contentment and gratitude is sincerely and regularly practised, the mind will be greatly protected against the temptation to be over-attracted to earthly things.

Guidance involves heart-management

The essence of this chapter is that the quest for God's guidance includes heart-management, watching out for and guarding against covetousness. Here, in summary form, are the five best antidotes:

1. Pray earnestly and self-searchingly for help, confessing your faults in this matter.

2. Practise self-denial, keeping a firm restraint on yourself. Do not spoil or pamper yourself, always choosing the best of anything, when something less may be more than adequate.

3. Be thoughtful, liberal and enthusiastic in your support of the Lord's work, making this a major priority in your financial plans. Carry it high on your heart!

4. Ensure that your greatest interests are spiritual, and not earthly, controlling the agenda of your thought-life.

5. Practise the art of Christian contentment, with daily gratitude and thanksgiving to God for all that he, in his providence and grace, has given you.

Some verses of Philip Doddridge reflect the burden of this chapter, being based on *Psalm 17.5*: 'Hold up my goings in thy paths, that my footsteps slip not.'

Beset with snares on every hand,
In life's uncertain path I stand;
Saviour divine, diffuse thy light,
To guide my doubtful footsteps right.

Engage this roving, treacherous heart,
O Lord, to choose the better part;
To scorn the trifles of a day,
For joys that none can take away.

Then let the wildest storms arise;
Let tempests mingle earth and skies;
No fatal shipwreck shall I fear,
But all my treasures with me bear.

6
Imagining the Lord's Interventions

'For God hath not given us the spirit of fear; but of power, and of love, and of a sound mind' *(2 Timothy 1.7)*.

HOW WE VIEW and talk about God's dealings with us from day to day can have a considerable effect upon our openness to his guidance in the great decisions of life. Many Christians have picked up a manner of thinking and speaking known as pietistic speech, which is very damaging to the perception of genuine guidance. These friends constantly ascribe all kinds of everyday events to the special and direct intervention of the Lord, as though their lives were filled with minor miracles. They believe this way of speaking is 'spiritual', and just what the Lord wants to see in his people. However, it frequently leads to a form of spiritual 'super-stition' in which Christians interpret their perceived interventions by God as signals of guidance.

We acknowledge that the Lord does intervene in the lives of his people, and there are many times when our circumstances are overruled in an unmistakable way, so that we cannot fail to recognise the hand of the Lord. But this is quite different from reading guidance into a chain of minor coincidences and 'deliverances'. Some believers, intoxicated by the idea that God constantly works direct miracles in their lives, begin to think of themselves as super-Christians who sense the mind of the Lord. Their imagination becomes their king as they 'feel led' to do one thing or another, or say, 'The Lord told me this morning . . . ' or, 'The Lord wants me to tell you . . . '

All this obstructs genuine divine guidance, which requires a spiritual outlook coupled with sober, rational judgement, sanctified by humility. Because the habit of pietistic thinking and speaking can upset the perspectives of believers and fog the thoughtful seeking of guidance, we must briefly review its dangers.

It is worth noting that when Christians adopt the habit of pietistic thinking and speaking, they mainly focus on very little things, or entirely personal events, not *great* matters. Furthermore, these are usually *earthly* rather than *spiritual* matters, and most significantly, the Lord usually gives them good events, not hard or painful ones. We have heard people say, 'The Lord sent a bus for me this morning.' In circumstances of great need and in answer to prayer the Lord may intervene very kindly to help his people, but he is also training us to endure hardship by his wonderful grace. Many years ago the writer was told by an earnest Christian lady who had been making jam, 'The Lord was marvellous to me this morning! He prevented the jam from boiling over while I was out.' On another occasion someone said, 'The sun has shone today, just when I sent my coat to the cleaners. What a wonderful thing! It must have been the Lord who commanded the sun to shine for me today.'

We repeat that God certainly does overrule and intervene in the lives of his people, through prayer, helping us in many ways, and frequently we realise that we have accomplished things we could never have done by our own ability or strength. What believer has not had the experience of remembering some vital responsibility just at the critical moment? We were certain that the Lord had done it, and we gave him thanks and glory. But we should not forget that all that happens to us is according to his will and permission, whether large or small, good or unpleasant.

The *immediate* cause of any occurrence in our lives may be natural or human, as natural forces and processes (known as *second causes*) are allowed to affect our lives under God's supervision. Often the devil is permitted to influence affairs, as he did when Paul said – 'But Satan hindered us.' Frequently we ourselves, through our sin or foolishness, are the real cause of our bad circumstances, the authors of many of our own misfortunes, and the Lord permits it for our sanctification. God is sovereign, and nothing happens to us except by his consent and overruling, as we see from the opening chapters of *Job*. We must not drift into the idea that only small, earthly and good things are examples of his providence. Why should we single out life's happy surprises and coincidences as instances of God's work in our lives? Why not talk about the days when nothing remarkable happened, or about times of illness and failure? Does not God superintend all that happens to his children?

Here are some of the consequences of pietistic speaking, showing how it may distort our view of the Christian life and confuse any quest for guidance. Those who engage in it are likely to become very *subjective* in their spiritual lives, ever focused on what is happening to *them*. Further, because their minds are so focused on seeing interventions of God they become increasingly vulnerable to their own imagination. Some become 'yo-yo' or 'up-and-down' believers, whose assurance and peace is entirely dependent upon their seeing a constant flow of divine interventions in their lives. They watch almost superstitiously for little signs, rather than resting on the Word and the promises of God. Ultimately, their faith depends upon apparent coincidences and hopeful comforts, these being the chief evidence that God's hand is upon them.

The writer remembers a young man who was most unhappy about something his church proposed to do. The objective was wholesome, and much needed, and the church had proceeded on the basis of biblical principles, but no amount of reasoning could help this young man see the value of the project. Then someone happened to tell him about a very small event which had occurred in the initial stages of the project and which had cleared away a hindrance. The unhappy young man's face lit up at once, and, like a superstitious person who had found a lucky charm, he changed his opinion dramatically and totally. He had not been amenable to the *need* recognised by his church, but half an ounce of coincidence outweighed all his reservations. It is very possible that the small event that had made all the difference to his outlook was an intervention of the Lord, but it was never intended to be the exclusive, authoritative, decisive piece of guidance, and we have lost our way when we think only in these terms. It does not take much imagination to see the difficulties which many believers get into because they make similar coincidental or surprising occurrences the sole or chief basis of their guidance.

The famous words of *Romans 8* tell us – 'And we know that all things work together for good to them that love God, to them who are the called according to his purpose.' To achieve this he allows us, alongside our blessings, to be exposed to a lifetime of temptations, troubles, trials, sorrows, inconveniences, illnesses and failings, whether brought about by ourselves, the devil, or by natural circumstances. While we must experience these troubles and difficulties, the Lord weaves all the strands of life's experiences together, using them to chastise, strengthen and train, in short, to work our eternal spiritual good. Through trials the Lord may be rebuking us for some sin, or training us and improving our resilience and character for some future service. Equally, he may be stimulating our dependence upon him in prayer, or teaching us to be sensitive to the hardships of others, or simply reminding us that we should fix our affections on heavenly things and not attempt to get our satisfaction from the things of this world. When we are about to suffer minor discomfort because of the weather, or the late-running of a bus, it is not necessarily God's will that we should be delivered from that problem. Everything that goes 'wrong' is part of our training for Heaven.

In *Romans 8*, where it is said that all things work together for our good, we do not read about earthly comforts, but about being kept close to Christ in the midst of – 'tribulation, or distress, or persecution, or famine, or nakedness, or peril, or sword'. We do not deny that God makes remarkable provisions for his people, but judging from the detailed narratives of Luke and Paul, such interventions are generally connected with times of special need, such as when we are on some important service for the Lord, or when he is being especially sympathetic to us in some severe trial.

Before hastily ascribing all comforts to God we should remember that the devil can also bring 'good' into our lives (by the Lord's permission), such as when he tries to distract us from the Lord's service with comforts, benefits, flatteries, and great earthly opportunities. Satan may also arrange for us to be given gifts, pleasant surprises, or comforts in order to entice us into worldly friendships, alliances or careers.

The devil uses 'wiles' (that is *strategies*) says Paul in *Ephesians 6*, and King Solomon also points to the strategy of flattery as a prime tool in the onslaught on the soul of the believer (the adulterer in *Proverbs*, for example, working by flattery and fair speech). From the beginning of his offensive against believers Satan has used pleasant things to deceive. The trouble with friends who ascribe a constant stream of minor benefits to God's direct intervention, is that they do not seem to realise that the Lord works to lift their interests above earthly, minor and domestic things, to make them more concerned about their part in the work of Christ, and the progress of the Gospel. He would hardly shower minor personal miracles upon them contrary to his own training objectives. In the first chapter, reference was made to *Matthew 6.25-34*, where the Lord gave the rule which his disciples should follow, saying:

> Take no thought for your life, what ye shall eat, or what ye shall drink; nor yet for your body, what ye shall put on. Is not the life more than meat, and the body than raiment? . . . But seek ye first the kingdom of God, and his righteousness . . . Take therefore no thought for the morrow . . .

The apostle Paul tells us that God's power and blessing flowed most of all when he was weak and disadvantaged. He tells us about the thorn in his flesh permitted by God in order to counteract the pride he may have experienced as the result of the great revelations given to him, then he concludes –

> Most gladly therefore will I rather glory in my infirmities, that the power of Christ may rest upon me. Therefore I take pleasure in infirmities, in reproaches, in necessities, in persecutions, in distresses for Christ's sake: for when I am weak, then am I strong *(2 Corinthians 12.9-10)*.

Paul also shows that believers are often called to endure hostility and unreasonableness, saying, 'Alexander the coppersmith did me much evil: the Lord reward him according to his works: of whom be thou ware also' *(2 Timothy 4.14-15)*. Whatever Alexander did, the apostle was not delivered from his bitter hostility, and he warned believers of all ages to watch out for such a man. In the same passage Paul refers back to his first trial in Rome when no one stood with him, remembering that – 'Notwithstanding the Lord stood with me, and strengthened me' *(2 Timothy 4.17)*.

In *2 Corinthians 11* the apostle describes his 'stripes above measure', how he had been imprisoned many times, beaten with rods, stoned, shipwrecked three times, and suffered danger, treachery, exhaustion, sleeplessness, pain, extreme hunger, thirst, cold, and exposure. None of these trials had been averted, and so the story of his life contrasts sharply with the accounts of non-stop, divinely provided comforts which some speak so excitedly about today.

Troubles came frequently to Paul because he served the Lord, and although these were not always averted, he was always strengthened to withstand them until God's moment of deliverance came. We notice also that when God intervened to deliver Paul from his first imprisonment, it was specifically for a spiritual purpose, namely – 'that by me the preaching might be fully known, and that all the Gentiles might hear: and I was delivered out of the mouth of the lion' *(2 Timothy 4.17)*.

Significant interventions give assurance

As we asserted at the beginning of this chapter, a selective, trivialising view of God's providential dealings with us profoundly affects our approach to guidance, distorting our Christian perspectives, and causing us to read all the wrong messages into God's providences. From earliest times God's people were taught to take a far higher view of God's conspicuous providential overrulings showing that they were given for spiritual purposes.

Two classic Old Testament events illustrate this, both taking place at Mahanaim, a place in old Gilead which received its name from Jacob, who saw there one of the most uplifting sights of his life, recorded in *Genesis 32.1-2*. Fearful of his approaching meeting with Esau, he was met by the angels of God, and when he saw them he said, 'This is God's host: and he called the name of that place Mahanaim.' The name means 'a double camp' or 'a double host', indicating that the thousands of angels seen by Jacob resembled a double army.

Why, at this particular time in his life, should he be privileged to see the army of Heaven which cared for him? Clearly, it was to reassure him, and equally, to teach him to distinguish between his *earthly* circumstances and his *spiritual* lot. As he thought about his earthly situation he might well feel fearful and depressed, facing an immense trial. But when, for a moment, the curtain of time and sense was drawn aside, he caught a glimpse of his spiritual, heavenly status and privileges, realising he was a child of the heavenly King, attended by those who minister to the heirs of salvation. So today, God's conspicuous interventions are designed partly to remind us of our *spiritual* privileges; but there is more to it than this.

Nearly a thousand years later Mahanaim was the site of another outstanding demonstration of God's power to intervene and bless. This occurred just as King David brought to an end his sorry retreat from Absalom, and decided to take a stand and defend his kingship (the event being recorded in *2 Samuel 17*). As soon as he turned from despondency to obedience and trust, Mahanaim proved true to its name once again. This time, no double host of angels appeared, but the power of God became visible in another way when three wealthy landowners, moved by the hand of God to come to the aid of David's destitute army, supplied provisions on a scale which he could never have expected or imagined, and the way was set for a great victory.

God also blesses his people with many remarkable interventions in the major battles of faith and service. When we are going forward for the Gospel, then he marshals and moves both people and events to bring about his purposes. David was not delivered from the hardships of the battle, nor from the crushing heartache of personal grief over his rebellious son, but God moved mightily to preserve and prosper his own work and witness. Once David returned to where he should have been, prayed to God, and dedicated himself to the battle, God encouraged him with the tremendous evidence of overruling power.

We believe that our God intervenes and provides for his people in all things, but we must particularly look for these blessings in the great concerns of life, and especially in service for the Lord. Sometimes the blessing comes in the form of *inner strength*, as with Paul in Rome, and sometimes as a great blaze of assurance, as when Jacob saw the double host of angels. If we really commit ourselves to the Lord, sever all entanglements with worldly living, and seek to put him first, then we shall experience many evident interventions, and be able to say: 'The best of all is – God is with us!'

However, we must be extremely careful what we say to others, for the evidences of God's presence should humble us, and not spur us to pride and vainglory. As far as all the lesser comforts and benefits are concerned, we shall praise God for them all, although we cannot necessarily tell when God is merely permitting the natural course of events to take place, or when he is intervening directly.

To summarise, constant pietistic speaking about the Lord's supposed direct interventions in all the minor matters of our lives frequently leads to an over-confident presumption that he is behind everything we think or do. Then the attitude of humble and open enquiry so vital to the seeking of guidance is undermined. Also, this seemingly super-spiritual line of speech so often leads us to be more concerned about personal and even material aspects of life than about the major matters of holiness, obedience and service.

7
Guidance and Loyalty to the Local Church

'But now hath God set the members every one of them in the body, as it hath pleased him. And if they were all one member, where were the body? But now are they many members, yet but one body. And the eye cannot say unto the hand, I have no need of thee: nor again the head to the feet, I have no need of you' *(1 Corinthians 12.18-21).*

ONE OF THE GREATEST problems reported in the life of local churches today is the lack of a deep sense of loyalty on the part of many members. Sometimes when believers decide where they would like to live, or where they will apply for new jobs, almost the last matter put into the reckoning is their commitment to their church. Pastors everywhere affirm that Christians are too often guided by material and personal considerations, and not by any sense of duty and loyalty to their fellowship.

Is it possible that our criteria for such decisions are out of line with the Lord's? What if he wants our present church commitment to be a dominating priority, and we relegate it to a matter of small importance? Will this not make all ideas of guidance an empty delusion? Clearly, it is vital for us to know the 'rating' our existing church commitment should be given on our scale of priorities. This chapter will show that some of the other guidance factors are subservient to this.

The writer knows of a 'pioneer' church where some years ago nine or ten couples committed themselves together to establish a witness in a new town destitute of evangelical light. Within three years, all but two of the couples had moved off elsewhere. The reason? Most had moved to get higher status and more lucrative jobs within their professions. Apparently these moves were not all absolutely essential, but the free choice of people who felt no deep bond of loyalty to the local 'body of Christ' in which God had placed them. Even though it seemed inevitable that their leaving would press their fledgling church to the brink of disaster, these couples considered their careers and incomes their chief priority.

A 'low' or 'high' view of the church?

How have such believers come to regard their ties with their local church so lightly? Obviously they have not really understood the Bible's teaching about the local church. Perhaps they have not realised what is meant by 'the body of Christ'. They think that the church is like a supermarket chain, or a network of banks. No one would decide against moving from one town to another because they were rather attached to their supermarket or bank branch. Suitable facilities exist almost wherever they may go.

What is the local church in our estimation? Is it merely a company of Christians conveniently gathered together for worship and instruction, or is it something special in God's sight? Has God chosen its members, organised the distribution of gifts and abilities, and called those individuals to be committed to each other to serve him and to live as a unique family? Does God require a special loyalty within the local church?

Liberty is the 'in' word today. For some believers, loyalty to any particular congregation smacks of restriction, legalism, and a mechanical interpretation of Christian duty. Loyalty is regarded as quenching the spirit of liberty. Yet the New Testament is clear in its portrayal of the local church as a company of believers very strongly related together in bonds of love *and loyalty* and service. The local church is much greater than a haphazard collection of believers. It is a spiritually integrated family vested with unique privileges and authority to carry out the commands of its Head, the Lord Jesus Christ. A local church is the object of his delight, and he is especially protective towards it.

The local church is – as Paul says repeatedly in *1 Corinthians 12* – *one body*. In the eighteenth verse he says, 'now hath God set the members every one of them in the body, as it hath pleased him.' In other words, God has designed each congregation. Paul goes on to say – 'There should be no schism in the body.' He then says that God has organised the distribution of capacities so that every member is of importance to the body. We therefore conclude that if any are removed, other than by the design and overruling of the Lord, some vital quality will be missing. The members care and feel for one another to the extent that when one suffers, all the others suffer also (verses 25-26). The *congregation* has a special place in the purposes of God.

Ephesians 4.16 describes the organic unity of the congregation using the most close-knit illustration available – that of the physical body. Under the direction of the Head – 'the whole body fitly joined together and compacted by that which every joint supplieth, according to the effectual working in the measure of every part, maketh increase of the body unto the edifying of itself in love.'

The idea of joints and limbs being freely interchangeable between different bodies is unthinkable. The notion that a knuckle or elbow could unilaterally migrate to another body is ludicrous. The illustration of the body shows how seriously God takes his sovereign right to place his people in particular churches, according to his overall plan. Our God insists that we see our lives and our service *in the context of the particular church family to which he appoints us.* Verses such as this place great emphasis on a group of people being edified together, so that they relate together in love, mutual care and dedicated service for the Lord, showing forth God's power and grace.

In the light of the fact that the New Testament urges us to have a high view of the local church, how is it that so many evangelical believers have come to take such a low view? One possible reason is that they misunderstand our evangelical rejection of earthly church power. They notice that we repudiate human domination, such as church government by centralised councils or hierarchies, and that we shun human priesthood, emphasising instead the priesthood of all believers, and the direct access to the Saviour for all who seek him. However, they carry the liberty of individual believers too far, and come to think that the believer should not subordinate himself in any way to a church. They see no obligation at all, regarding the congregation as nothing more than a practical arrangement to facilitate worship and instruction.

Obviously, if the local church is no more than this, then it has no more claim upon anyone's allegiance than a school or university or supermarket or bank. As long as believers contribute towards the benefits they receive, they should not be inconvenienced or required to make sacrifices for their local church.

While it is true that the local church has no dominating authority over the lives of its members (other than to apply the standards clearly announced in the Bible), God insists that his people should feel obligated to their churches in a special way, striving to worship and serve as a co-ordinated unit, a society of people called to prove him in the closest harmony. And they are to be loyal to their church until God himself calls them elsewhere by unmistakable guidance.

All this is taught in the various biblical pictures or metaphors of the church, particularly those of the body, the Temple building, and the family unit. Church members are pictured as *integral* and *irremovable* parts performing vital functions. God's special regard for the local church as a cohesive unit is to be seen in the warning of *1 Corinthians 3.16-17*, where Paul writes to that congregation: 'Know ye not that ye are the temple of God, and that the Spirit of God dwelleth in you? If any man defile *[or destroy]* the temple of God, him shall God destroy; for the temple of God is holy, which temple ye are.'

Should the believer move?

In the light of the special status and significance of a local church, the permanent move of a believer from one church to another should only take place as the result of the clear overruling guidance of God. Later in this chapter we shall consider when loyalty is wrong, but in normal circumstances the believer's first thought must always be, 'God has called me to be loyal to my present community. Can I therefore be sure that it is his will that I should move? Am I really being called somewhere else? Is there clear evidence of his leading, supported by circumstantial guidance and having taken account of the counsel of my brothers and sisters in the Lord?'

Often Christian people are closely attached to their church, making a valuable contribution, but then a practical problem arises which appears to make moving necessary. It may be that their firm is moving to another town, or that employment prospects are much better somewhere else, or that their present area is prohibitively expensive for housing, and prices are much lower in another region of the country. None of these problems should *immediately* lead us to feel that moving is the only solution. One of the great assurances of the Christian life is that although we are frequently tried and tested by problems, often seemingly insurmountable ones, when we turn to God in prayer, he intervenes and helps us. The history of grace is a story of wonderful, often astounding, provisions from the Lord. However, some believers, the moment a problem arises of the kind mentioned, assume that it can be resolved only by uprooting and moving. They panic, and see only radical solutions, and they do not seriously ask the Lord to provide for them so that they can remain loyal to their church work. All this is very sad, with churches receiving heavy blows because members do not attempt to prove their Lord.

Some pastors have felt this very keenly, especially those ministering in new towns or inner-city areas into which Christian people hardly ever seem to move, but out of which they move very readily. Many churches in these areas 'generate' converted souls for the churches of other places, while they themselves remain as struggling causes. Did the Lord design it that way? Did he intend that his people should be totally dominated by practical problems?

Obviously, we must not expound loyalty in such a way as to obstruct the ways of God. We recognise that the sovereign Lord may move his people from one church to another. He is our heavenly General who knows the whole battlefield and all his various outposts or churches along the front line. He may call people who are settled in one church to uproot and transfer to another, just as in the New Testament we see the Lord moving his servants from one place to another, sometimes by sweeping large numbers out of communities by persecution, and sometimes by other means.

As a general rule, when circumstances arise which could remove us from our church, our first hope should be that the Lord intends us to prove him where we are. It is only after we have sincerely sought a solution, and exhausted all reasonable possibilities, that we should become open to moving away. How can we expect to be led in the 'right way', if we have no respect for the Lord's revealed priorities? The seeking of guidance must be rooted in a biblical value system, and this includes the duty of loyalty and commitment to the congregation in which God has set us. If a church is going seriously wrong in honouring biblical essentials, believers may be compelled to leave (as we show from page 114).

Encouraging loyalty

Two concepts arising out of the expression 'the body of Christ' should help us to develop the supportive, devoted attitude which we ought to have for our local church. This magnificent term (used in *1 Corinthians 12.27*) may refer in Scripture both to the entire, world-wide Church of Christ, and to an individual congregation. As we have seen, the term speaks of a harmonious, closely organised unit, with interdependent parts and limbs. But it also speaks of a person's *presence*. Just as we are present in a place when our body is there, so Christ is seen in the world by his church. Every (spiritual) local church is his representative body in the world.

Surely, then, the local church, as his representative body, must be treated with the utmost respect and consideration. As members, *we* are the body of Christ! Whatever we do for his representative body, we do for him and to him. Whatever we fail to do for the church, we fail to do for him. If I am lazy or indifferent toward my church – the body of Christ – I am lazy and indifferent to him. If I am disloyal to his body, I am disloyal to him. How can I hurt the body of Christ, or abuse it? How can I lightly leave or forsake it?

To further stir our loyalty to the local church there is a second idea suggested by the term 'body of Christ'. It is that of the *sanctity of life*. The word 'body' reminds us that the local church is a living thing. Supposing we see a person lying in the street, injured and bleeding; what do we do? Do we just pass by? If we do, we will afterwards feel sick and desperately ashamed, because there is within everyone a powerful respect for life, and we cannot betray that instinctual responsibility for the preserving of life without paying a price.

As Christians, we should possess a similar instinct for the health and well-being of the body of Christ, the local church. Viewed spiritually, it is a precious, living body, Christ being alive in its members, having bound them together to represent him in the world. How can we allow it to be hurt? How can we bear to see limbs torn out? The world allows and encourages abortion, which is an outrage against the sanctity of human life, but the indifference shown by some believers to the body of Christ is to some degree a similar outrage in the spiritual realm.

When church members uproot and move as though their place in the body of Christ is of no significance, it is because they have lost their sense of awe and respect for the local church as the body of Christ. What a precious and important thing the congregation is! It is far, far more than a 'convenient arrangement'. It is something to which we owe special love, loyalty and service, so long as it remains a worthy church.

Wrong motives for leaving

When the next trial arises in our lives, will we have the right priorities? In *Romans 16.10* Paul salutes Apelles, who was 'approved in Christ', which means that he had gained the victory in a great test or trial. He had come through that trial on the Lord's side, proving his power in his situation. Many fall in the time of trial without even a struggle, and consequently they may suffer years of unhappiness without real spiritual usefulness. Some have gone into a spiritual wilderness because matters of career or location became the biggest influence in their lives, causing them to abandon their place in the service of the Lord.

In times of trial or decision, we need to search our hearts to see what desires are really influencing us. We know of people who have moved from the inner city because they did not care for built-up areas, and longed for green fields and beauty. The assumption of these friends was that other Christian city-dwellers adored the polluted air and grimy buildings. Clearly if all members of inner-city churches followed the natural desire to flee to more pleasant districts there would be no evangelical churches left in our most densely populated areas.

Countless Christians stand fast in other undesirable and

unattractive locations, remaining for the sake of their local church and its testimony. Where in the Bible do we read that the first rule of guidance is that we are to seek the most congenial and attractive surroundings? It is the worldling who makes his own pleasure and enjoyment his first priority, but we are to stay or go wherever the Lord positions us, realising that trials and temptations await us in an 'Eden' just as much as in a 'Babylon'.

There are other factors also which carry people away from their churches unnecessarily. Every pastor has experience of members who have moved away from their fellowship because they had some besetting weakness they would not control. Their spiritual lives suffered, they became unhappy, and eventually decided that the fault was not in them but in their church. They began to sulk and complain, and soon became convinced that they were not receiving spiritual food, help or fellowship. Eventually they left the church, but not because the Lord had led them on. A high and worthy view of the local church may have helped them not to turn against their church, but they did not have such a view, and the church soon became a punch-bag for the release of tensions and dissatisfaction.

C. H. Spurgeon may well have been describing this in *Sermons in Candles*. Alongside an engraving of a very odd-shaped candle, unable to fit into any holder or stand, he wrote:

> I know persons who cannot get on anywhere; but, according to their own belief, the fault is not in themselves, but in their surroundings. I could sketch you a brother who is unable to do any good because all the churches are so faulty. He was once with *us*, but he came to know us too well, and grew disgusted with our dogmatism and want of taste. He went to the Independents who have so much more culture, breadth, and liberality. He grew weary of what he called 'cold dignity'. He wanted more fire, and therefore favoured the Methodists with his patronage. Alas! he did not find them the flaming zealots he had supposed them to be: he very soon outgrew both them and their doctrines, and joined our most excellent friends, the Presbyterians.
>
> These proved to be by far too high and dry for him, and he became rather sweet upon the Swedenborgians, and would have joined them

had not his wife led him among the Episcopalians. Here he might have enjoyed the *optium cum dignitate*, have taken it easy with admirable propriety, and have even grown into a churchwarden; but he was not content; and before long I heard that he was an Exclusive Brother!

There I leave him, hoping that he may be better in his new line than he has ever been in the old ones. 'The course of nature could no further go': if he has not fallen among a loving united people now, where will he find them? Yet I expect that as Adam left Paradise so will he ultimately fall from his high estate.

An unsettled member's heart-searching must be ready to unearth unsavoury motives. Why would we want to leave our church? Sometimes people become disenchanted through thinking of themselves more highly than they ought to think, becoming very upset because their perceived talents are not sufficiently recognised, and they are not given early respect or office. They soon think they will be much better off in another (much 'better') church, and having lost their biblical loyalty, they may eventually make their move.

When loyalty is challenged

Although some people have failed in their loyalty to their church, countless others have proved the Lord in a marvellous way. The practice of loyalty to *biblical priorities* has brought them a series of wonderful provisions and blessings. Over the years we have heard often of accommodation being found, mortgages becoming unexpectedly available, employment needs being met, and a host of other provisions also. Sometimes it transpires that the Lord really is leading a believer to a new church 'posting', but often he provides so that they may stay where they are.

It may be that to remain in one's church will entail a loss of employment status, or some other cost, and we should ask ourselves, 'Am I ready for this?' We should remind ourselves that the history of the church is full of the loyal sacrifices of the Lord's people. Years ago, in time of war, men left their families to go and fight for their country, and many in fear and trembling performed heroic deeds. Many were cut down in their youth for the defence of the realm. But what cause could be more vital or glorious than that of the Lord of hosts, and the battle for everlasting souls? Yet we hear of believers who say, 'I would never put my career prospects at risk. I must do whatever my company demands, and go wherever promotion or advancement dictates.' The mighty grace of God brings new values and emotions into the life of a true convert, and we must take care not to lose these values as we go on in the Christian life. We must be *all* for Christ, and for his cause and his church.

It is good for us to keep in mind the fact that all believers at some time are likely to be subjected to the devil's attempts to shift them from the church fellowship where God has placed them. There will be many difficulties and trials for all, and the more they seek to serve the Lord, the more they will encounter them. We all need great tenacity, and a deep sense of belonging to our church. Most believers who have been especially used by God for the building up of their fellowship have at some time been subjected to intense pressures to uproot and relocate elsewhere. Perhaps these trials were given so that they might prove the Lord's provisions for them, and be all the more certain of their 'posting'. Satan is constantly trying to spoil churches by taking believers out of the 'element' in which God has placed them. He is constantly tempting God's people to seek greener pastures elsewhere.

What about those new-town young couples referred to at the beginning of this chapter, who walked out on an infant church so easily? Were they people of loyalty, commitment, sacrifice and courage? One wonders where they are now. Are they enjoying high academic or commercial positions? Are they well established in beautiful homes with fine cars parked in their driveways?

In seeking guidance, let us recognise that when the Lord sets us in a sound church, it is a divine appointment, and we must honour and respect that with all our strength. We are not free agents, and should never be moved by whims. When it is God's time to move us elsewhere, we must be fully and sincerely satisfied that he is really directing and overruling.

This chapter has said nothing about special cases, such as students, or even ministers of the Gospel. The existence of a sound church for Christian service is a key factor in choosing a college, but a study course in another city does not come within the scope of a permanent move. Ministers may be called by God from one sphere of ministry to another. We acknowledge that there are many legitimate reasons for Christians to be on the move, and the Lord is frequently the author of our moves, but the responsibility of honouring primary biblical loyalties has been too widely ignored in these days of high 'mobility', to the great hurt of churches and individuals.

When loyalty is wrong

Although loyalty to the local church is a biblical duty, there are circumstances in which loyalty is misplaced, and believers should leave. The painful irony is that some Christians show little loyalty to their church when God commands them to *cleave to it*, and amazing loyalty when God tells them to *leave it*. To know when loyalty is commanded, and when it is not, is a crucial aspect of divine guidance. Thousands of believers have remained trapped in apostate denominational churches where the Truth has long been derided and compromised, because they misunderstood loyalty and placed it before Truth.

The fact is that in his Word God constantly calls his people out of dead and unworthy churches, but numerous believers appear not to notice. They deprive themselves of sound ministry, strengthen the hands of false teachers (the Lord's enemies), and lose years of fruitful service by remaining in unsound churches. The biblical command that we should stay clear of all false teaching and apostasy is not merely negative, but is a positive and constructive act of spiritual obedience, safeguarding the true Gospel message and protecting the doctrinal purity of the people of God. The work of the Gospel is seriously hampered by the fact that many of the Lord's people are spread thinly around in compromised or completely dead and apostate churches. If they would only regroup to stand behind *sound,* Gospel-preaching churches, these would be vastly more effective. The biblical call to separate from error is God's own call to his people, and to obey it is a response of love leading to positive blessing.

Consider the many texts in which we are told not to associate with churches and ministers who deny the fundamentals of the true faith, such as the infallibility of the Bible, and the doctrine of salvation by faith alone. In *Romans 16.17* Paul commands that we 'mark them which cause divisions and offences contrary to the doctrine which ye have learned; *and avoid them.*' Should we worship and work in churches with false teachers? Should we listen to and support ministers and clergy who do not wholeheartedly believe and teach the Gospel? The inspired apostle writes: 'Though we, or an angel from heaven, preach any other gospel unto you than that which we have preached unto you, let him be accursed' *(Galatians 1.8).* Apostate churches and preachers are (says Paul) 'the enemies of the cross of Christ' *(Philippians 3.18).* The apostle John (in *2 John 10-11*) lays a solemn charge upon us, saying of ministers and clergy who reject true evangelical doctrine – 'If there come any unto you, and bring not this doctrine, receive him not into your house, neither bid him God speed: for he that biddeth him God speed is partaker of his evil deeds.'

Are we assisting non-evangelical teachers? Have we not realised that in God's sight we are assisting his enemies? The scriptures quoted are God's authoritative commands to us, telling us to leave wrong church connections. We should not say, 'Well, I'll think about it, and see if the Lord leads me.' He *has* led us already.

In *1 Timothy 4.1* we are warned that 'in the latter times some shall depart from the faith, giving heed to seducing spirits, and doctrines of devils.' False teaching will enter many churches, and take them over. How should true believers respond? Says Paul, 'If any man... consent not to wholesome words, even the words of our Lord Jesus Christ, and to the doctrine which is according to godliness... from such withdraw thyself' *(1 Timothy 6.3-5)*. We are to 'shun' false teaching *(2 Timothy 2.16)*.

The command to believers to keep themselves completely apart from Bible-denying error is also expressed in *2 Corinthians 6.14-17*:

> Be ye not unequally yoked together with unbelievers: for what fellowship hath righteousness with unrighteousness? and what communion hath light with darkness? and what concord hath Christ with Belial? or what part hath he that believeth with an infidel? and what agreement hath the temple of God with idols? for ye are the temple of the living God; as God hath said, I will dwell in them, and walk in them; and I will be their God, and they shall be my people. Wherefore come out from among them, and be ye separate, saith the Lord, and touch not the unclean thing; and I will receive you.

The purpose of our reviewing these biblical passages is to show that God has already provided ample guidance on this issue. The matter is already settled for us in Scripture. If a church teaches or allows fundamental error, or associates supportively with those that do, we have a duty to appeal for repentance and correction, and if there is no response, to leave.

These scriptures apply not only to churches, but also to a Christian Union in our college or firm if that society has non-evangelical committee members and speakers. Nor should we support evangelistic crusades that have committee members and ministers on the platform who are opposed to evangelical Truth, and which refer their 'converts' to unsound churches. In all these matters we already have clear guidance in the Word. Other issues also call for withdrawal from churches and CUs, such as their use of contemporary worship styles, contrary to *James 4.4*, or the adoption of charismatic ways, following post-biblical visions. (The author covers these in *Worship in the Melting Pot, The Charismatic Phenomenon* and *The Healing Epidemic.*)

When loyalty is wrong toward sound churches

Are there any circumstances in which believers ought to leave doctrinally sound churches? Sadly, there are church failings which are so serious that Christians have a duty to withdraw if the situation cannot be corrected. Even though a church may wholeheartedly believe the fundamental doctrines of the Bible, it may fall into such sin that it is no longer fit or qualified to function as a church, and no longer entitled to the loyalty of its members. We see this in the *Book of Revelation* where the church at Ephesus was told that if it did not repent of its sin it would have its 'candlestick' or 'lampstand' (its status as a true church) taken away. Here are three areas of church misconduct which involve such serious disobedience to God that dedicated Christians must withdraw – if the church refuses to address the situation:

1. First, *if a church refuses to exercise discipline* when serious offences are committed by members, then we have a duty to protest, and if the church refuses to obey God's Word, to leave it. 'Have no fellowship,' says the Lord through Paul, 'with the unfruitful works of darkness, but rather reprove them' *(Ephesians 5.11).* The New Testament insists that the purity of the church is taken seriously, and *1 Corinthians 5* shows the necessity of this.

2. Secondly, *if a church shows no inclination to obey the great commission* and engage in Gospel work, and nothing can be done to stir it up to obedience, believers may well have a duty to leave that church. A local church must proclaim the Gospel. If this primary function is ignored, then the church forfeits the loyalty of true-hearted members. How can they be expected to waste their lives in lazy, heartless or disobedient churches? Why should they be rendered fruitless because their church is not interested in the Saviour's highest work?

3. Thirdly, *if a church ignores the standards of God's Word* by allowing the use of worldly and carnal styles of worship and evangelism, then true believers are bound to experience a great crisis of conscience. How can they cleave to a church which corrupts holy things and makes its members participate in ungodly worship contrary to *James 4.4* – 'Know ye not that the friendship of the world is enmity with God? whosoever therefore will be a friend of the world is the enemy of God.' Loyalty to the Lord and his commands in such areas certainly comes before loyalty to the local church.

All three examples mentioned here cancel out the duty of loyalty to a church, regardless of the fact that it may be sound in basic doctrine.

Where such problems do not exist, however, we must believe that God calls us to a church, and commands us to be loyal to it. We should regard ourselves as permanent limbs or parts of that body until he moves us, and have a readiness to be utterly faithful to any sound and active fellowship to which God shall call and 'post' us. The Christian life is not a life of selfish individualism, but a life to be spent as a fellow labourer and fellow soldier in that unit of believers where God intends us to be.

> *Lord, from whom all blessings flow,*
> *Perfecting the church below,*
> *Steadfast, may we cleave to thee,*
> *Love the powerful union be;*
> *Bind our willing spirits, join*
> *Each to each, and all to thine,*
> *Lead us into paths of peace,*
> *Harmony and holiness.*
>
> *Move and actuate and guide;*
> *Various gifts to each divide;*
> *Placed according to thy will*
> *Let us all our work fulfil;*
> *Never from our service move,*
> *Needful to each other prove;*
> *Use the grace on each bestowed*
> *Fashioned by the hand of God.*
>
> *Charles Wesley*

8
Guidance in Church Decisions

'Beware of false prophets, which come to you in sheep's clothing, but inwardly they are ravening wolves. Ye shall know them by their fruits. Do men gather grapes of thorns, or figs of thistles? Even so every good tree bringeth forth good fruit; but a corrupt tree bringeth forth evil fruit' *(Matthew 7.15-17).*

W E MUST CONTINUE to relate the subject of guidance beyond our personal lives to the great issues which confront our churches. As we saw in the previous chapter, God sets us in congregations to serve him alongside other believers, and requires loyalty and intelligent commitment of us. This is God's scheme, not ours, and it would be selfish to want God's guidance for personal decisions, while being indifferent to the life and problems of his churches. In the following pages we turn from personal guidance to church guidance, for we must play our part in seeking the Lord's will at both levels.

Tragically, believers do not always pay much attention to the wider scene, and to what churches at large are doing, and this can have horrific consequences as we see from the history of evangelicalism in the United Kingdom. A hundred years ago Britain teemed with Bible-believing churches, chapels, missions and assemblies, fervently reaching the lost, but the last hundred years has witnessed the closure of thousands of them, and the surrender of many more into the hands of people who do not believe in an inspired Bible. Virtually all the evangelical theological colleges that once trained men to preach the Gospel have also been lost to theological liberalism.

The speed and extent of the decline in evangelical witness has been astonishing. False doctrine blew through the churches like a forest fire, swiftly bringing all the historic denominations under the domination and control of non-evangelicals. First, theological colleges of all the historic Protestant denominations were taken over by those who rejected the fundamentals of the faith, corrupting future ministers and clergy, then congregations were swayed by the new generation of non-evangelical preachers, abandoning the old faith. Today we count ourselves fortunate to have one or two Gospel-preaching churches in the average larger town.

The questions we must ask are: Did rank and file believers do anything to stop this decline, or did they allow it? And if they failed to stem the tide of error, are we doing any better today? Is the decimation of evangelical witness continuing through our indifference or lack of discernment? What are the newest, latest threats to what remains of evangelical churches?

There is no doubt that in very many churches, sound Christians put up no fight against the repudiation of evangelical Truth in their denominations, nor is there any doubt that the same failure to take a stand continues today with Satan's current onslaught. The defenceless state of evangelicalism today is commonly sustained by an almost incredible misinterpretation of Christ's command, 'Judge not, that ye be not judged' (Matthew 7.1). Many years ago this writer experienced this after giving a sermon in which there was a warning about an example of false teaching. A visiting hearer approached me with a 'word from the Lord', rebuking me for having included negative criticism in the sermon. Opening his Bible, this visitor read out in a solemn, judicial way: 'Judge not, that ye be not judged.'

My reprover believed that we should never exercise judgement or discernment as Christians, but behave naively in the face of error. The Bible and sound doctrine must never be defended, and we are to close our eyes when tares are being sown among the wheat, or when wolves come among the flock. Is this the correct interpretation of the Lord's words – 'Judge not, that ye be not judged'? Of course not, because vigilance and discernment is constantly commanded in the Bible, and particularly by the Lord himself. The extraordinary idea that we must put our minds in hibernation while the churches are corrupted by error, is one of the most costly mistakes ever made in the history of biblical interpretation. How long can evangelicals survive if they ban sound judgement and discernment?

If in *Matthew 7.1* the Lord commands us not to discern and judge, then he contradicts himself – which is impossible – for in the same chapter he says, 'Beware of false prophets' – a command which obviously involves making a judgement. It should be obvious that the Lord's words do not forbid the right use of our faculties to assess teachers and methods, and to watch out for danger, folly and sin. The Lord's words 'judge not' must be understood by the words that immediately follow: 'Judge not, *that ye be not judged.*' His purpose was to condemn *hypocritical* fault-finding, not the right and proper exercise of Christian discernment. He condemned those who passed judgement on others for committing the very errors they themselves were guilty of. He says, in effect, 'Do not judge another when you deserve to be judged for the same fault.' J. C. Ryle explains the passage perfectly:–

> Our Lord does not mean that it is wrong, under any circumstances, to pass an unfavourable judgement on the conduct and opinions of others. We ought to have decided opinions. We are to 'prove all things'. We are to 'try the spirits'. Nor does he mean that it is wrong to reprove the sins and faults of others until we are perfect and faultless ourselves. Such an interpretation would contradict other parts of

the Scripture. It would make it impossible to condemn error and false doctrine. Heresy would flourish. What our Lord means to condemn is a censorious and fault-finding spirit; a habit of passing rash and hasty judgement; a tendency to magnify the errors and infirmities of our fellows, and make the worst of them.

To make it absolutely clear that this important verse does not contradict the duty of making sound judgements, we need only read on to *Matthew 7.3-5*, where we are given the picture of a man with a very grave and obvious fault (the beam in his eye), criticising a brother whose fault, by comparison, is a splinter or speck. 'Thou hypocrite,' says the Lord, 'first cast out the beam out of thine own eye; and *then* shalt thou see clearly to cast out the mote out of thy brother's eye.' Once the hypocrite has purged his own offence by seeking God's help to rid himself of it, he certainly has a duty to exercise discernment in addressing the smaller offence of his brother. The threat of false teaching getting into the local church is so serious that the Lord describes it (in the very same chapter) in terms of a pack of wolves getting in amongst grazing sheep. Once in, the wolves will tear and kill the sheep, scattering the flock, and this is exactly what has been allowed to happen in so very many churches.

Biblical commands to detect error

In *1 Timothy 4.1-6* we are told that a good minister of Jesus Christ is one who reminds his church 'that in the latter times some shall depart from the faith, giving heed to seducing spirits, and doctrines of devils.' He must not only have sound judgement himself, but he must train his people to exercise the same faculty. Timothy is also warned about those 'having a form of godliness, but denying the power', from whom he is to 'turn away', but how could he do this without exercising judgement and discernment? He is further commanded to train 'faithful men' to succeed him in his work. How would he know who they were without discernment? (See *2 Timothy 2.2*.) Great care and discernment is to go into the selection of leaders and teachers in the churches of God, a powerful warning from Paul being recorded in *Acts 20.28-31*:

> Take heed therefore unto yourselves, and to all the flock, over the which the Holy Ghost hath made you overseers . . . For I know this, that after my departing shall grievous wolves enter in among you, not sparing the flock. Also of your own selves shall men arise, speaking perverse things, to draw away disciples after them. Therefore watch, and remember, that by the space of three years I ceased not to warn every one night and day with tears.

Paul exercised constant vigilance in protecting the churches and the Truth, and some people had to be rejected because of their apostasy. To Timothy, Paul wrote the following words commanding clear judgement and discrimination:

> This charge I commit unto thee, son Timothy, according to the prophecies which went before on thee, that thou by them mightest war a good warfare; holding faith, and a good conscience; which some having put away concerning faith have made shipwreck: of whom is Hymenaeus and Alexander; whom I have delivered unto Satan, that they may learn not to blaspheme *(1 Timothy 1.18-20)*.

The apostle John's command to give no co-operation to opponents of biblical doctrine (also mentioned in the previous chapter), reads –

> Whosoever transgresseth, and abideth not in the doctrine of Christ, hath not God. He that abideth in the doctrine of Christ, he hath both the Father and the Son. If there come any unto you, and bring not this doctrine, receive him not into your house, neither bid him God speed: for he that biddeth him God speed is partaker of his evil deeds *(2 John 9-11)*.

Who is it today who denies that Jesus Christ (God the Son) has come in the flesh? Obviously, atheists, cults, and non-Christian religions deny Christ's deity, but so do many who claim to be Christian ministers. They say they believe Christ is God, but if they think that he was unable to perform miracles, that he was not infallible, and that he did not know what he was talking about when he spoke of atonement and new birth, and such matters, they clearly do not really believe that he was the living God from Heaven. True belief in the deity of Christ includes unwavering acceptance of his divine power, and of all his utterances, and so John's words condemning those who deny that Christ has come in the flesh, apply to present-day theological liberals. We are commanded by his words to have no fellowship with, and to give no recognition to, the overwhelming majority of ministers in the historic denominations, because this is exactly their position.

The letter of *Jude* (verses 3-4) provides this exhortation:

> Beloved, when I gave all diligence to write unto you of the common salvation, it was needful for me to write unto you, and exhort you that ye should earnestly contend for the faith which was once delivered unto the saints. For there are certain men crept in unawares, who were before of old ordained to this condemnation, ungodly men, turning the grace of our God into lasciviousness, and denying the only Lord God, and our Lord Jesus Christ.

The Bible commands us to have spiritual fellowship only with fellow believers in the Gospel. Concerning those who teach 'another gospel', we should certainly be concerned about their spiritual state, and wish to bring them to salvation, but we must never extend to them recognition as true Christians, nor join with them in Christian work, because to do this is to break the clear command of Scripture and confirm them in the delusion that they are true Christians.

Today, however, evangelicals are being urged by some of their leading preachers to join hands with Catholics, especially charismatic Catholics, even though they worship Mary, celebrate mass, and deny the central doctrine of justification by faith alone.[1] Catholics are described by these leaders as truly saved Christians, even though they have no belief in or experience of the new birth, and obey the

---

1 For example: *The Nottingham Statement*, to which 1000 Anglican evangelical clergy assented in 1977, under the chairmanship of John Stott, which included the declaration: 'Seeing ourselves and Roman Catholics as fellow-Christians, we repent of attitudes that have seemed to deny it.' (Church Pastoral Aid Society, London.)

authority of Rome rather than the Word of God.

The importance of judgement and discernment in maintaining the doctrinal and moral soundness of churches is constantly emphasised in the New Testament, an example being *Titus 3.10*, 'A man that is an heretic after the first and second admonition reject.' How can we obey this text without exercising discernment? *Hebrews 12.15* tells us to watch carefully to ensure that the fellowship is not put at risk by seriously backslidden, apostate or embittered members. Once again we ask, how can this be obeyed without discernment? The excommunication of the Corinthian sinner is an obvious biblical example of how church judgement is to be applied in the case of a serious moral lapse.

The battle for biblical doctrine in the main British church denominations was lost before World War II, as by this time the overwhelming majority of Anglican, Methodist, Baptist and Congregational churches were no longer evangelical. For a time, in the post-war decades, the remnant of Bible-believing churches, most of which were outside the old denominations, maintained a good stand, but by the 1970s new strategies were being deployed against them by Satan. While continuing to insinuate anti-evangelical teaching, he began a major offensive in which godless *activities* would be introduced, activities which would gradually corrupt and bring about the spiritual decline and fall of churches. Innovations were introduced into worship and witness such as worldly entertainment-style music, the shallow Gospel of the seeker-sensitive churches, and more recently the sub-biblical teaching of the 'emergent church' movement. Will we accept them blindly, as so many believers accepted theological liberalism, or will we apply scriptural judgement to the various new methods of worship and service, in accordance with the command of *1 Thessalonians 5.21-22*, which reads: 'prove [test] all things; hold fast that which is good; abstain from all appearance of evil'? Tragically, in many churches these destructive influences sweep in unchallenged.

We should expect Satan's ancient policy of infiltrating churches to be operating today. Paul warns of 'false brethren' coming into the church by stealth, to spy and to 'bring us into bondage' with subtle and false teaching *(Galatians 2.4)*. He did not give an inch of ground to such teachers, refusing to recognise their ministry and their viewpoint, unlike many believers today who think that it is unnecessary to take a stand for the Truth. May we pray for help to become a discerning generation, jealous for God's Truth, God's glory, and God's great and gracious name.

Men and women are needed, and particularly young men and women, who will abandon the fickle, undiscerning way of accepting anything and everything, and take their stand on the authoritative Word of God, ready to safeguard and proclaim both the message and the lifestyle of true servants of Christ. Only then will churches fulfil their role as 'the *pillar* and *ground* of the truth', and only then shall we see once more the blessing of God in the conversion of many souls.

May our desire for personal guidance always include a willingness to be guided by God's Word in matters of the church, particularly its separateness from false teaching, and the spirituality and purity of its worship and witness. The guidance of God comes in a special way to those who live for the spread of the Gospel, and for the safeguarding of the Truth. The Lord himself has said so, through the lips of Isaiah:

> And if thou draw out thy soul to the hungry, and satisfy the afflicted soul; then shall thy light rise in obscurity, and thy darkness be as the noonday: and THE LORD SHALL GUIDE THEE CONTINUALLY, and satisfy thy soul in drought, and make fat thy bones: and thou shalt be like a watered garden, and like a spring of water, whose waters fail not. And they that shall be of thee shall build the old waste places: thou shalt raise up the foundations of many generations; and thou shalt be called, The repairer of the breach, The restorer of paths to dwell in *(Isaiah 58.10-12)*.

May this be the experience of every reader!

Appendix
Tests for Amusements and Recreations

by Richard Baxter (1615–1691)

Adapted from the great Puritan's work, *A Christian Directory* (1673),
Part 1 – Christian Ethics, Chapter 10, 'Directions against sin in sports
and recreations'.

I F YOU WISH TO AVOID the sin and danger of unbiblical amusement masquerading as acceptable recreation, you must understand what acceptable or lawful recreation is, together with its legitimate purpose. No wonder Christians sin, if they do not know what is right. Without doubt some amusement and recreation is lawful, indeed, necessary, to some people. Lawful recreation is the enjoyment of some natural thing, or participation in some activity which is not forbidden, for the stimulation of the natural spirits. It may be for the use of the mind or the exercise of the body. It is some pleasurable activity or exercise, ultimately intended to fit the body and mind for their normal duty to God.

Amusement, sport and recreation are special terms. We do not call arduous labour by such terms, though it may be better for us and more necessary. Nor do we call every enjoyment by these terms, for eating and drinking may be pleasurable, and holy things and duties may be delightful, yet they are never termed sports or recreations. It is the imaginative faculty that is chiefly delighted by amusements.

Tests for biblical lawfulness

All the following factors are necessary to render an amusement, sport or recreation lawful, and the lack of any one of them will prove it to be unlawful.

1. The genuine purpose or intention behind your indulging in it must be to fit you for your service to God. It must help you to function better either in your work, or in his worship, or for some work of obedience in which you may please and glorify him: *1 Corinthians 10.31* says, 'Whether therefore ye eat, or drink, or whatsoever ye do, do all to the glory of God.' A lawful recreation must be a means fitly chosen and used to this end. If it has no ability to improve us for God's service in our ordinary callings and duty, it cannot be to us a lawful recreation (though it may be lawful to another person to whom it is a real help).

2. All recreations are unlawful which are for their own sakes preferred before our callings.

3. All recreations are unlawful which are used only to delight a carnal imagination, and have no higher end than to please the sickly mind that loves them.

4. All recreations are unlawful which hinder and spoil our fittedness for the duties of our callings, and for the service of God; or, which, putting the benefit and hurt together, hinder us as much or more than they help us.

5. All recreations are unlawful which take up any part of the time which we should spend in greater works. In this category are all those that are unseasonable (as on the Lord's Day, or when we should be at prayer or any other spiritual service or duty).

6. All recreations that take up more time than is reasonable for a recreation are equally unlawful.

7. If an activity is profane, such as making sport of holy things, it is a mocking of God. It is wickedness demanding God's heaviest punishment, and cannot be lawful.

8. All recreations which wrong other people are unlawful. (This includes the activities of stage players and comedians who ridicule others to their injury.)

9. It is also sinful to make fun of the sinful ways of others, or to act them ourselves, which is common with comedians and other profane wits.

10. Unclean, obscene stage plays and recreations are unlawful, in which filthiness is represented without due expression of its odiousness, or with obscene words or actions. To Christians, *Ephesians* *5.3-4* applies: 'But fornication, and all uncleanness, or covetousness, let it not be once named among you, as becometh saints; neither filthiness, nor foolish talking, nor jesting.'

11. Those amusements are unlawful which involve the multiplying of worthless words, engaging the participants in foolish, needless, unprofitable chattering.

12. Those amusements are sinful which tend to provoke in ourselves or others lust, swearing, cursing and railing, and fighting and squabbling.

13. Those amusements and recreations are sinful which involve covetousness, to win money from others; or that tend to stir up covetousness in those you play with.

14. Cruel recreations also are unlawful: such as taking pleasure in watching duellers, fighters, or any that abuse each other; or any animals that are made to needlessly torment each other.

15. A recreation is unlawful if it is too costly, for we are God's stewards, and must be accountable to him for all we have. It is sinful to spend needlessly on amusement.

16. Lastly, if you have the choice of various recreations before you,

you must choose the fittest: and if you choose one that is less fit and profitable, when a fitter might be chosen, it is sin; even though that which you chose would have been lawful, if you had no other.

By all this it is easy, for example, to judge the lawfulness of our common stage plays.

What is a fit recreation? It is either the body or the mind that needs recreation most. Either you are sedentary people, or those who are physically applied. If the former, then it is the body that has most need of exercise and recreation. In this case, to sit at sedentary amusements or recreations, instead of exercising your bodies, is to increase the need of exercising them. It does you much more harm than good.

If, however, you are hard labourers, and need rest for your bodies and recreation for your minds, or are sick, so that you cannot use bodily exercise, then surely a hundred profitable 'exercises' are at hand which are more suitable to your case. You have books to read (including the Word of God) which can increase your knowledge in history, geography, and arts and sciences.

Questions to be asked

Here are some questions to ask yourself from time to time about your recreations, or those which may draw you:

1. Do you think that either Christ or his apostles used stage plays or similar entertainments and amusements, or ever sanctioned or encouraged addiction to them?

2. Does not your conscience tell you when your delight is more in your amusements than it is in God? Such recreations (those we love more than the things of God) in no way increase our delight in God, but take it away.

Do you not feel what a plague certain pleasures are to your affections – how they bewitch, befool you, and take you out of love with holiness, and make you unfit for anything that is good?

3. Do you bestow as much time in praying and reading the Word of God and meditating on it, as you do in your sports and recreations? Do you not know the value of those precious hours which you play away?

4. Would you be found at stage plays or vain amusements when death comes? Would you not rather be found at some holy or profitable labour?

5. Will it be any comfort to you when you are dying, to think of the time which you spent in plays and vanities?

6. Dare you pray to God to bless your sports and amusements to the good of your soul or body? Would not your conscience tell you that this would mock God?

7. If you are sure that you sin not in your games or sports, either by excess or addiction or neglect of spiritual duties, are you sure that your companions do not? If you say, 'We are not bound to keep all other men from sin,' I answer – You are bound to do your best towards it; and you are bound not to contribute willingly to their sin. If Paul would never eat flesh while he lived rather than make a weak person offend, should not your sports be subject to as great charity?

If you know what sin is, and what it is to save or lose one's soul, you will not aid and abet other men's sin, nor so easily contribute to their plight. In such cases, 'we then that are strong ought to bear the infirmities of the weak *[that is, to help them, as we do children in their weakness]*, and not to please ourselves *[to their hurt]*. Let every one of us please his neighbour for his good to edification *[that is, prefer the edifying of another's soul, before our own pleasure]*. For even Christ pleased not himself.' If Christ lost his life to save men from sin, will not you lose your sport for it?

8. What kind of people are they that are most addicted to games and plays, and what kind of people are they that avoid them, and are against them? With whom are these activities most identified? Judge wisely!

Choosing a recreation

Here are some helpful counsels about choosing a recreation:–

1. When you understand the true nature and purpose of lawful recreation, try to determine just how much and what sort of recreation is needful to you in particular. In this you must have respect, (a) to your bodily strength; (b) to your mind; (c) to your type of work. And when you have determined what and how much is needful and appropriate to help you in your duty, allow it its proper time and place, as you do your meals, and see that you do not allow it to encroach upon your duty and service.

2. Try normally to join profit and pleasure together, that you lose no time. It is a sin to idle away any time which we can turn to better account.

3. Watch against inordinate, sensual delight, even in the most lawful activity. Excess of pleasure in any such 'small' or lesser activity of life is very corrupting to the mind. It puts it out of relish with spiritual things; and turns it from God, and Heaven, and duty. To this end keep a watch upon your thoughts and fantasies, that they run not after sports and pleasures. Else you will be like children that are thinking of their sport, and longing to be at it, when they should be at their books or business.

4. Avoid the company of revellers, game-crazy people, and similar time-wasters. Come not among them, lest you be ensnared. Usually, amusements rate as foolishness to serious men; and they say of this mirth, as Solomon, 'it is mad' (Ecclesiastes 2.2). It is great and serious subjects which make serious men.

5. Be zealous and apply yourself to your calling and spiritual service. Laziness breeds a love of amusement. When you must please your flesh with ease, then it must be further pleased with vanities.

6. The sickly and the melancholy (who are usually least inclined to sport) have much more need of recreation than others, and therefore may allow it more time than those in health and strength.

7. Be much more severe in regulating yourselves in your recreations, than in censuring others for using some sports which you mislike. For you know not perhaps their case, and reasons, and temptations. An idle, time-wasting, sensual sporter, everyone should look on with pity as a miserable wretch.

If you are sedentary, walking or some honest, bodily exertion that joins pleasure and profit, is a fit kind of exercise for you.

If you are a labouring person, and need only pleasure for your mind, you can take pleasure in Scripture, in holy conference, or in good books. We have herbs and flowers and trees and beasts and birds and other creatures to behold. We have fields or gardens or meadows or woods to walk in. We have our near relations to delight in; our wives or children, and our friends. We may talk with good, and wise, and cheerful people, about things that are both pleasing and edifying to us.

God has given us a world of lawful pleasures. But stage plays are, at best, very questionable, and most are to be condemned as unlawful. Should one who fears God and loves his salvation choose so doubtful a recreation in preference to so many undoubtedly lawful ones?

And you must know what a time-wasting sin *excessive* leisure is. Suppose the activity is lawful: is it lawful to give so many hours to it, as if you had neither souls, nor families, nor other responsibilities or service to perform?

For myself, when my mind needs recreation, I have a variety of relaxing and invigorating books, and friends, and business to do that. And when my body needs it, the hardest labour that I can bear is my best recreation. Walking serves instead of games and sports as profitable to the body, and more to my mind. If I am alone, I may improve the time in meditation. If I am with others, I may improve it in profitable, cheerful conference.

I condemn not all sports or games in others, but I find none of them all to be best for myself; and when I observe how far the temper and life of Christ and his best servants were from such recreations,

I avoid them with the more suspicion. And besides, I note that most people, by instinct, view ministers with distaste when they see them pursuing recreations.

Church Membership in the Bible

61 pages, paperback, ISBN 978 1 870855 64 8

Christ has designed a 'home' or family for his people, described in these pages as an accomplishment of divine genius. This is a magnificent subject, vital to spiritual growth and blessing and also to our service for the Saviour.

This book answers many questions about churches and church membership in New Testament times. Next to having a real walk with Christ and knowing the doctrines of the faith, membership of a good church has a powerful formative influence on the believer's life.

Faith, Doubts, Trials and Assurance

139 pages, paperback, ISBN 978 1 870855 50 1

Ongoing faith is essential for answered prayer, effective service, spiritual stability and real communion with God. In this book many questions are answered about faith, such as –

How may we assess the state of our faith? How can faith be strengthened? What are the most dangerous doubts? How should difficult doubts be handled? What is the biblical attitude to trials? How can we tell if troubles are intended to chastise or to refine? What can be done to obtain assurance? What are the sources of assurance? Can a believer commit the unpardonable sin? Exactly how is the Lord's presence felt?

Dr Masters provides answers, with much pastoral advice, drawing on Scripture throughout.

The Faith
Great Christian Truths
119 pages, paperback, ISBN 978 1 870855 54 9

There is nothing like this popular, non-technical sweep through key themes of the Christian faith, highlighting very many inspiring and enlivening points. It often takes an unusual approach to a topic in order to bring out the full wonder and significance. It is designed to be enjoyed by seasoned Christians, and also by all who want to explore the great features of the faith, and discover the life of the soul.

CONTENTS:

The Mysterious Nature of a Soul	The New Birth
What God is Actually Like	Why the Resurrection?
The Fall of Man	Prophecies of Resurrection
The Three Dark Hours of Calvary	The Holy Trinity

Worship in the Melting Pot
148 pages, paperback, ISBN 978 1 870855 33 4

'Worship is truly in the melting pot,' says the author. 'A new style of praise has swept into evangelical life shaking to the foundations traditional concepts and attitudes.' How should we react? Is it all just a matter of taste and age? Will churches be helped, or changed beyond recognition?

This book presents four essential principles which Jesus Christ laid down for worship, and by which every new idea must be judged.

Here also is a fascinating view of how they worshipped in Bible times, including their rules for the use of instruments, and the question is answered – What does the Bible teach about the content and order of a service of worship today?

Do We Have a Policy?
Paul's Ten Point Policy for Church Health & Growth
93 pages, paperback, ISBN 978 1 870855 30 3

What are our aims for the shaping of our church fellowship, and for its growth? Do we have an agenda or framework of desired objectives? The apostle Paul had a very definite policy, and called it his 'purpose', using a Greek word which means – a plan or strategy displayed for all to see.

This book sets out ten policy ideals, gleaned from Paul's teaching, all of which are essential for the health and growth of a congregation today.

Not Like Any Other Book
Interpreting the Bible
161 pages, paperback, ISBN 978 1 870855 43 3

Faulty Bible interpretation lies at the root of every major mistake and 'ism' assailing churches today, and countless Christians are asking for the old, traditional and proven way of handling the Bible to be spelled out plainly.

A new approach to interpretation has also gripped many evangelical seminaries and Bible colleges, an approach based on the ideas of unbelieving critics, stripping the Bible of God's message, and leaving pastors impoverished in their preaching.

This book reveals what is happening, providing many brief examples of right and wrong interpretation. The author shows that the Bible includes its own rules of interpretation, and every believer should know what these are.

The Lord's Pattern for Prayer
118 pages, paperback, ISBN 978 1 870855 36 5

Subtitled – 'Studying the lessons and spiritual encouragements in the most famous of all prayers.' This volume is almost a manual on prayer, providing a real spur to the devotional life. The Lord's own plan and agenda for prayer – carefully amplified – takes us into the presence of the Father, to prove the privileges and power of God's promises to those who pray.

Chapters cover each petition in the Lord's Prayer. Here, too, are sections on remedies for problems in prayer, how to intercede for others, the reasons why God keeps us waiting for answers, and the nature of the prayer of faith.

God's Rules for Holiness
Unlocking the Ten Commandments
139 pages, paperback, ISBN 978 1 870855 37 2

Taken at face value the Ten Commandments are binding on all people, and will guard the way to Heaven, so that evil will never spoil its glory and purity. But the Commandments are far greater than their surface meaning, as this book shows.

They challenge us as Christians on a still wider range of sinful deeds and attitudes. They provide positive virtues as goals. And they give immense help for staying close to the Lord in our walk and worship.

The Commandments are vital for godly living and for greater blessing, but we need to enter into the panoramic view they provide for the standards and goals for redeemed people.

The Mutual Love of Christ and His People
An Explanation of the Song of Solomon
115 pages, paperback, ISBN 978 1 870855 40 2

The courtship of the *Song of Solomon* provides fascinating scenes and events designed to show the love of Christ for his redeemed people, and theirs for him. Here, also, are lessons for Christians when they become cold or backslidden, showing the way to recover Christ's presence in their lives.

Prophecies of Christ abound in the *Song*, together with views of the bride's destiny, as she prepares to cross the mountains into eternal glory, where the greatest wedding of all will take place.

Joshua's Conquest
Was it moral? What does it say to us today?
119 pages, paperback, ISBN 978 1 870855 46 4

Rooted and grounded in love for the Lord, Joshua was utterly faithful, wonderfully stable, and scrupulously obedient. The book of the Bible that bears his name is a magnificent anthology of events to challenge and inspire God's children in every age.

This is a book for reading, rather than a commentary. Its aim is to bring out the spiritual message of *Joshua* for today, and also to explain some of the 'problem' portions and passages which evoke questions on, for example, the morality of so much killing, and whether God was responsible for hardening the hearts of the Canaanites.

In Joshua we find the holiness and mercy of God fully displayed, and numerous encouragements for the spiritual life.

Men of Destiny

166 pages, illustrated paperback, ISBN 978 1 870855 55 6

The 40th anniversary edition of this immensely popular collection of great Christian biography. Here are the lives of fourteen remarkable people having in common a personal spiritual experience which changed and moulded them. Ideal for giving as a gift to unsaved friends, and useful for preachers and youth leaders. Includes:

The Tsar who Crushed Napoleon – Tsar Alexander Pavlovich
Bowers of the Antarctic – Lieut 'Birdie' Bowers
Discoverer of Chloroform – Sir James Simpson
The Word's Most Notorious Counterfeiter – Alves Reis
The Story of 'Fiddler Joss' – Joshua Poole
Leader of the Lords – Viscount Alexander of Hillsborough
Sailor, Deserter, Slave-Trader – John Newton
The Man Behind the Red Cross – Jean Henri Dunant
Dawn Breaks Over Europe – Martin Luther
Burned at the Stake – Bilney, Tyndale & Latimer
The Making of a King – Alfred the Great
Hero of Malta – Lieut-General Sir William Dobbie

Men of Purpose

157 pages, illustrated paperback, ISBN 978 1 870855 41 9

The companion volume to *Men of Destiny*. This brings into one illustrated volume eleven great lives, all with an experience of personal conversion to God. Includes:

The Dawn of Electricity – Michael Faraday
The Founder of a Food Empire – Henry J Heinz
A Composer's Journey – Felix Mendelssohn
The 'Lord Apostol' – Lord Radstock
Genius at Work – James Clerk Maxwell
The Heart of a Hymnwriter – Philip P Bliss
Brewer who Renounced a Fortune – Fred Charrington
Spearhead into the Unknown – Lord Kelvin
The Prodigal Poet – James Montgomery
Pioneer of Power – Sir John Ambrose Fleming
Island of Despair – Daniel Defoe

The Charismatic Phenomenon
Co-author: John C. Whitcomb
113 pages, illustrated paperback, ISBN 978 1 870855 01 3

The authors describe the purpose of the sign-miracles and revelatory gifts of New Testament times, and their precise nature. Were they intended to be ongoing in the life of the church? Numerous questions are here answered, such as, 'What exactly are the greater works of *John 14.12*?' and 'Are the signs following, referred to in *Mark 16*, for today?' This work has been helpful to many thousands, having passed through numerous printings in English, and having been translated into many other languages.

The Healing Epidemic
227 pages, illustrated paperback, ISBN 978 1 870855 00 6

This book traces the origins of the upsurge of healing ministries, then takes each of the main arguments used by healers in support of their methods, and shows how each is mistaken. Important facts are provided about demonology, showing just what demons can and cannot do. It is then proved from Scripture that the sign-gifts have ceased. A chapter describes how *James 5* should be implemented in churches today. Two important chapters present the biblical commands that the conscious mind should always be alert and rational for all worship and spiritual service. Included is an assessment of miraculous healing by a leading British doctor who was for many years a professor at Leeds University Medical School, the late Professor Verna Wright.

For other Wakeman titles please see www.wakemantrust.org